THE IDEA OF EUROPE

The Idea of Europe

Enlightenment Perspectives

Texts selected by
Catriona Seth and Rotraud von Kulessa

Translated by Catriona Seth et al.

OpenBook Publishers

https://www.openbookpublishers.com

Open Book Classics Series, vol. 7 | ISSN: 2054-216X (Print); 2054-2178 (Online)

ISBN Paperback: 978-1-7837-4378-0
ISBN Hardback: 978-1-7837-4379-7
ISBN Digital (PDF): 978-1-7837-4380-3
ISBN Digital ebook (epub): 978-1-7837-438-10
ISBN Digital ebook (mobi): 978-1-7837-438-27
DOI: 10.11647/OBP.0123

Cover image: Cannibal Queen, *Colours* (2011), https://www.flickr.com/photos/cannibal_queen/5791733736. Cover design by Heidi Cobourn.

All paper used by Open Book Publishers is SFI (Sustainable Forestry Initiative), PEFC (Programme for the Endorsement of Forest Certification Schemes) and Forest Stewardship Council(r)(FSC(r) certified.

Printed in the United Kingdom, United States and Australia
by Lightning Source for Open Book Publishers (Cambridge, UK)

Contents

Didier Robert de Vaugondy, *Universal Atlas* (1737), map no.14.
© Bibliothèques-Médiathèques de Metz ATR 5132.

Preface

25 March 2017 marked the 60th anniversary of the Treaty of Rome, which laid the foundations for the future European Economic Community. In 1957, representatives of six countries—the three Benelux nations, West Germany, France and Italy—met in the Palazzo dei Conservatori, on the Capitol, to set up an international agreement. The twelve signatories, who were academics, lawyers and diplomats, some of whom had been members of the resistance or imprisoned during the war, aimed to reinforce the ties between their lands and, through commercial exchanges, to stabilise the continent. Not quite six decades later, the United Kingdom voted in a referendum to leave the European Union at a time when the consortium's twenty-eight member states (twenty-seven after Brexit) are being buffeted by increasing criticisms of the project and of the ideals which led to its formation. Scepticism seems to be the order of the day, wherever you turn your eyes. It is sometimes fuelled by populisms which seek, through a return to particularisms and nationalisms, to pander to a part of the population which globalisation has left feeling stranded.

Observing the current challenges—many of them political—by which different European countries are confronted, European researchers who work on the eighteenth century decided to turn to earlier expressions of common values and past evocations of questions which remain valid today. Many men and women of letters envisaged the future of the continent in particular to try and bring peace to Europe. The texts which follow, signed by major Enlightenment figures such as Rousseau, Montesquieu, Voltaire, Kant, Hume or Germaine de Staël, as well as those whom history has forgotten, showcase the reflections of thinkers—mainly from the long eighteenth century—about Europe, its history, its diversity, but also that which unites a very varied geographical group. They underline the historical origins of a projected European Union with texts like the 1713 *Project for Perpetual Peace in Europe*. The Abbé de Saint-Pierre, its author, attempted to propose an innovative solution to the violent convulsions suffered by his country—France—and by neighbouring states at the time of the war of Spanish succession: a union, rather than a balance of powers, and the association of Turkey or the Maghreb within commercial networks, rather than their exclusion. He speaks out in favour of what he calls a 'Treaty of *Supreme Policy*, or *European Arbitrage*, to keep all the parts of Europe united in a single Body'.

Like him, there are others who proposed ideas, recounted past events, or imagined possible developments. Sometimes they are wrong, as hindsight shows. On occasion, they express ideas which we do not always share or which now appear outdated. One thing they have in common is to have wanted to think about what makes Europe, in its diversity and singularity, and about ways to envisage its future and to celebrate its diversity. Often they have wished, beyond party politics, for closer ties among European nations and greater intellectual and commercial collaboration.

If, at the start of the nineteenth century, the idea of the existence of national characters and identities remained a potent one, thinkers like Germaine de Staël—to whom the Prince de Ligne wrote: 'It is truly to you that one could write as an address: *To the genius of Europe*' —or Victor Hugo, who considered an American-style federal union, frequently stressed the importance of European unity to defuse future conflicts. In his famous speech to the 1849 Peace Congress, as he foresaw a time when a war between Paris and London, Saint Petersburg and Berlin or Vienna and Turin would seem as absurd and impossible as between Rouen and Amiens or Boston and Philadelphia, Victor Hugo heralded a radiant future: 'A day will come when France, you Russia, you Italy, you England, you Germany, you all, nations of the continent, without losing your distinct qualities and your glorious individuality, you will merge into a superior unity and you will constitute European fraternity just as Normandy, Brittany, Burgundy, Lorraine, Alsace, all our provinces merged into France'. He called what corresponds to the vision of contemporary federalists the 'United States of Europe'. He imagined technical progress going hand-in-hand with this fraternal advance: 'Thanks to the railways, Europe will soon be no larger than France was in the Middle Ages! Thanks to steamboats, it is now possible to cross the Ocean more easily than one used to cross the Mediterranean! Soon man will travel round the earth like the Gods of Homer crossing the heavens in three strides. In but a few years, the electric wire of concord will surround the globe and embrace the world.'

Hugo's optimism would have been sorely challenged by the rise of populism and fear of foreigners which at times compromise relations in current western societies, but it still resonates with those of us who refuse to be beaten by the spirit of suspicion and identify with a common heritage and ambitions, celebrating our differences as occasions for sharing and learning. At a time when we need to rethink Europe, its aims and contours, it is surely wise to look at what men and women proposed in the past. We should listen to Edward Gibbon, for whom the true philosopher thinks on the scale of Europe and does not allow himself to be limited by national frontiers, or examine Benjamin Constant's suggestions of ways to bring about the end of wars. The aspirations of enlightened thinkers, even when they are marked by the period in which they were conceived or by an outmoded eurocentrism, deserve a hearing. We are their heirs. Those who come after us will be fully justified in asking us to account for this intellectual inheritance.

This anthology is the result of an international collaboration. Its English version is the product of a crowdsourced translation, mainly thanks to the enthusiasm and talents of Oxford students and their tutors who met the challenge in record time with good humour and great skill.[i] The texts offer diverse approaches and ideas. They can be read in any order. The book can be shared without moderation throughout Europe and beyond. Its original version was in French.[ii] There will soon be a German translation too!

---

i   Extracts that are not derived from English-language editions have been translated by the contributors to this volume The spelling has been modernised.

ii   Rotraud von Kulessa and Catriona Seth (eds.), *L'idée de l'Europe au Siècle des Lumières* (Cambridge: Open Book Publishers, 2017), https://www.openbookpublishers.com/product/610/lid-e-de-l-europe-au-si-cle-des-lumi-res

We would like to extend our warm thanks to the colleagues, students and friends who made this possible by their invaluable contributions. Nicolas Brucker (Metz), Denis de Casabianca (Marseille), Carole Dornier (Caen), Fabio Forner (Verona), Marie-Claire Hoock-Demarle (Paris), Juan Ibeas (Vitoria), Frank Reiser (Freiburg), Ritchie Robertson (Oxford and Göttingen), Lydia Vázquez (Vitoria), the Société française d'étude du XVIIIᵉ siècle, the University of Augsburg and the University of Oxford were involved from the start.

A Note on the English Version

After the January 2015 terrorist attacks in Paris, the French Society for Eighteenth-Century Studies (SFEDS), horrified by the events and the climate of suspicion and fear which was being promoted in some parts of society, drew up an anthology of Enlightenment texts on the theme of Tolerance and sold it at a loss-making nominal price through newsagents in order to reach out to a wide audience. Caroline Warman, from Jesus College, Oxford, told me this was a fantastic achievement. When I suggested it would be even better if it could circulate more widely, for instance, by means of translations, she immediately offered to take the responsibility for crowdsourcing English versions of the texts. Thanks to students from all across the University of Oxford and their tutors, this was achieved and the book was launched on the first anniversary of the Parisian killings.[iii]

Many of us who study languages or speak more than one tongue are among those who feel that the European ideal remains a valid one, though it has been increasingly under attack. We wanted to show that questions about the degree of cooperation between countries, whether it should be formal or informal, which aspects of international law should be involved, but also the very natural tendency to adopt fashions—in dress, speech, mores—from our neighbours have been hotly debated for centuries.

The initial French anthology involved colleagues from various countries and with all sorts of research specialisms. The English version

---

iii   Caroline Warman, *et al.* (eds.), *Tolerance: The Beacon of the Enlightenment* (Cambridge: Open Book Publishers, 2016), https://www.openbookpublishers.com/product/418/ tolerance--the-beacon-of-the-enlightenment draws on Caroline Warman's experience and extends it: undergraduates, graduates and tutors, not only in French, but also in Spanish, German and Italian were all involved in preparing the extracts, many of which had never appeared in English. Others have been retranslated as an exercise out of which many of us gained both experience and enjoyment. Some of our wonderful students even translated texts from two different languages. All through the process I was struck by the enthusiasm and engagement of all the participants and I was at several points overwhelmed by offers or spontaneous translations—which sometimes meant a couple of drafts had to be merged for the one finally printed. These new translations do not pretend to offer definitive versions but they should allow the reader to discover interesting extracts and to reflect on past ideas, some of which still resonate nowadays.

So... three cheers for our wonderful students whose names follow: Thomas Abbott, Anousha Al-Masud, Gregory Alexander, Amber Bal, Lucy Balazs, Matthew Bannatyne, Frances Barrett, Sarah Barron, Demelza Batchelor, Lucasta Bath, Elicia Begg, Lily Begg, Anna Bellettato, Max Bhugra-Schmid, Imogen Bowyer, Roberta Brandter, Heather Cant, Anushka Chakravarti, Aidan Chivers, Lydia Cockburn, Cristina Conde Tkatchenko, Emma Corris, Flavia Cresswell-Turner, Joseph Cullen, Annabelle Dance, Lara Davies, Sarah Davies, Sam Davis, Holly Dempster-Edwards, Johanna Dieffenbacher, Catherine Drewry, Callum Duff, Niamh Elain, Florence Engleback, Amira Fateh, Xena Fawkes, Georgina Fooks, Rosie Fraser, Johanna Gewolker, Lucy Gibbons, Natasha Gibbs, Emma Gilpin, Miranda Gold, Alexander Goodchild, Conal Grealis, Megan Griffin, Isabella Grive, Marina Hackett, Elliott Harman, Victoria Hart, Imogen Haworth, Katie Holmes, Katherine Howell, Minying Huang, Megan Husain, Katarzyna Jaroszewicz, Seung Jung, Joseph Kelly, Charlotte Kendrick, Thalia Kent-Egan, Johanna von Kietzell, Beth Lamarra, Amy Layton, Caroline Lear, Joshua Lee-Tritton, Guosheng Liu, Jonah Lloyd, Isobel Losseff, George Mackenzie, Lily MacTaggart, Krystofer Mackie, Lydia Martin, Carmen Martínez, Ollie Matthews, Róisín McCallion, Lara McNeil, Waqas Mirza, Charlotte Molony, Lara Morgenstern, Samuel Moss, Emily Niblo, Jenna Noronha, Elizabeth Norton, Jemma Paek, India Phillips, Alma Prelec, Hannah Pritchard, Livvy Procter, Sam Purnell, Anastasia Putt, Nicole Rayment, Edward Rawlinson, Olivia Reneaud-Jensen, Adam Rhaiti, Colette

Rocheteau, William Rooney, Meris Ryan-Goff, Charlotte Ryland, Mobeen Salih, Harry Sampson, Bennett Sanderson, Jeanne Sauvage, Tina Shan, Marianna Spring, Hector Stinton, Georgiana Sutherland, Miriam Swallow Adler, Emily Taplin, Isabel Taylor, Samuel Thomas, Alexander Thompson, Martin Trpovski, Alexander Tucker, Anne-Jacqueline Uren, Laure Villa, Alex Ward, Lydia Welham, Emily Williams, Charlotte Willis, Iwo Wojcik.

The following Oxford colleagues also took part:

French: Sara-Louise Cooper, Tim Farrant, Jessica Goodman, Sarah Jones, Katherine Lunn-Rockliffe, Ian Machlachlan, Jake Wadham, Caroline Warman, Seth Whidden.

German: Alex Lloyd, David Murray, Charlie Louth, Kevin Hilliard.

Italian: Ela Tandello.

Spanish: Diana Berruezo Sánchez, Laura Lonsdale, Lucy O'Sullivan, Annabel Rowntree, Olivia Vázquez-Medina.

Fellows, tutors and/or students from the following Oxford Colleges were involved: All Souls, Christ Church, Exeter, Hertford, Jesus, Keble, Lady Margaret Hall, Lincoln, Magdalen, Merton, New College, Oriel, Pembroke, St Anne's, St Catherine's, St Edmund Hall, St Hilda's, St Hugh's, St John's, St Peter's, Somerville, Trinity, Wadham, Worcester.

We express our gratitude to Susan Seth (Saint-Arailles), Rose Simpson (Aberystwyth) and William Ohm (Toronto), who gave us extra support for our translations.

General thanks are also due to: Sandra Beaumont, Dena Goodman, Simon Kemp, Henrike Lähnemann, Ivana Lohrey, Stuart Parkes, Eva Rothenberger and, of course, all the staff at Open Book.

1. A Hymn for Europe

A poem by Friedrich Schiller (1759–1805),[i] the Ode to Joy, *associated with Beethoven's Ninth Symphony, has become the hymn for Europe after having been sung in concert halls and concentration camps, in Germany and far beyond its borders. A symbol of reconciliation, it bears witness at once to a common classical culture and to the aspiration towards future fraternity. Written in 1785, the text is marked by pietistic vocabulary, but also by its all-embracing enthusiasm.*

O Freunde, nicht diese Töne!
Sondern laßt uns angenehmere anstimmen
und freudenvollere.

Dear friends, do not play such music!
Let us rather take up melodies more pleasing
And more infused with joy.

Freude, schöner Götterfunken
Tochter aus Elysium,
Wir betreten feuertrunken,
Himmlische, dein Heiligtum!
Deine Zauber binden wieder
Was die Mode streng geteilt;
Alle Menschen werden Brüder
Wo dein sanfter Flügel weilt.

Joy, the gods' own spark of beauty
Daughter of Elysium
Fire-drunk pilgrims' solemn duty,
To your kingdom we shall come!
Your enchantment binds together
That which custom would divide,
All unite as friends and fellows
Where your gentle wings abide.

Wem der große Wurf gelungen,
Eines Freundes Freund zu sein;
Wer ein holdes Weib errungen,

He who casts the die with boldness
In great friendship shall rejoice,
Wins fair heart, thawed from its coldness

Mische seinen Jubel ein!
Ja, wer auch nur eine Seele
Sein nennt auf dem Erdenrund!
Und wer's nie gekonnt, der stehle
Weinend sich aus diesem Bund!

To our chorus join his voice.
He who calls but one soul his
In this, our great earthly sphere.
Only he who lives without is
Lost from Union, left in tears.

---

i   https://commons.wikimedia.org/wiki/File:Anton_Graff_Schiller_(1).jpg

    https://doi.org/10.11647/OBP.0123.02

Freude trinken alle Wesen   Joy, our Mother Nature's nectar,
An den Brüsten der Natur;   Drink from her consoling breast
Alle Guten, alle Bösen   Those who good or evil think
Folgen ihrer Rosenspur.   Are by her gentle hand caressed.
Küsse gab sie uns und Reben,   Nature's trail of vines we treasure,
Einen Freund, geprüft im Tod;   Friendship true, in death unflawed,
Wollust ward dem Wurm gegeben,   Lowly worms are given pleasure,
und der Cherub steht vor Gott.   And the cherub stands with God.

Froh, wie seine Sonnen fliegen   Joyful as the starry places
Durch des Himmels prächt'gen Plan,   Speeding on their endless way
Laufet, Brüder, eure Bahn,   Brothers, sisters, to your future
Freudig, wie ein Held zum Siegen.   As a hero wins the day.

Seid umschlungen, Millionen!   Let me now embrace you, people,
Diesen Kuß der ganzen Welt!   Let this kiss the world hear well;
Brüder, über'm Sternenzelt   Brothers, sisters, high above us,
Muß ein lieber Vater wohnen.   Must a loving father dwell.
Ihr stürzt nieder, Millionen?   Fall before him all you people
Ahnest du den Schöpfer, Welt?   World, who made you, love you well?
Such 'ihn über'm Sternenzelt!   Seek him in the stars above us
Über Sternen muß er wohnen.   In the heavens he must dwell.

Friedrich Schiller, 'Ode to Joy' (1785).

Read the text in the original language (1808 edition):
https://de.wikisource.org/wiki/Ode_an_die_Freude

2. Henry IV of France's Great Design

The Memoirs *of Maximilien de Béthune, Duke of Sully (1559–1641),[i] are the only account of the great design imagined by Henry IV (1553–1610), King of France from 1589 onwards: the confederation of a Christian Europe. This seemed so chimerical to the statesman that he hardly paid any attention the first time the monarch spoke of 'a political system through which the whole of Europe could be shared and led like a family'. The French sovereign believed none of the nations concerned could afford to reject the idea bearing in mind its advantages: 'The profit they will withdraw, above and beyond the inestimable value of peace, is far greater than that which they will have to spend'. In the context of the conflicts in Europe and, in particular, the aim of limiting the Spanish crown's power and appeasing religious conflicts, the French head of state developed his project in consultation with Queen Elizabeth I, in order to guarantee a solid peace for Europe. His project was not without importance for someone like the Abbé de Saint-Pierre in the eighteenth century.*

To render France happy for ever was his [the King of France's] desire; and she cannot perfectly enjoy this felicity, unless all Europe likewise partake of it; so it was the happiness of Europe in general which he

---

i   https://commons.wikimedia.org/wiki/File:Maximilien-de-Sully.jpg

laboured to procure, and this in a manner so solid and durable, that nothing should afterwards be able to shake its foundations. [...]

The troubles in which all the following years were engaged, the war which succeeded in 1595, and that against Savoy after the peace of Vervins, forced Henry into difficulties which obliged him to lay aside all thoughts of other affairs; and it was not till after his marriage, and the firm re-establishment of peace, that he renewed his thoughts upon his first design, to execute which, appeared then more impossible, or at least more improbable than ever.

He nevertheless, communicated it by letters to Elizabeth, and this was what inspired them with so strong an inclination to confer together in 1601, when this princess came to Dover, and Henry to Calais. [...] I found her deeply engaged in the means by which this great design might be successfully executed; and notwithstanding the difficulties which she apprehended in its two principal points, namely, the agreement of religions, and the equality of the powers, she did not to me appear at all to doubt of its success. [...]

We considered the death of the King of Spain as the most favourable event that could happen to our design, but it received so violent a shock by the death of Elizabeth, as had like to have made us abandon all our hopes. Henry had no expectation that the powers of the North, nor King James, the successor to Elizabeth, when he was acquainted with his character, would any of them so readily consent to support him in his design, as this princess had done. However, the new allies which he daily gained in Germany, and even in Italy, comforted him a little for the loss of Elizabeth. [...]

For what did he [Henry] hereby require of Europe? Nothing more than that it should promote the means by which he proposed to fix in the position, towards which, by his efforts, it for some time had tended. [...] By this he would have discovered the secret to convince all his neighbours that his whole design was to save, both himself and them, those immense sums which the maintenance of so many thousand soldiers, so many fortified places, and so many military expenses require; to free them for ever from the fear of those bloody catastrophes so common in Europe; to procure them an uninterrupted repose; and, finally, to unite them all in an indissoluble bond of security and friendship, after which they might live together like brethren, and reciprocally visit like good neighbours, without the trouble of ceremony, and without the expense of a train of attendants, which princes use at best only for ostentation, and frequently to conceal their misery. [...]

I am persuaded such an armament would have been so highly approved of by all these princes, that, after they had conquered with it whatever they would not that any stranger should share with them in Europe, they would have sought to joint to it such parts of Asia as were most commodiously situated, and particularly the whole coast of Africa, which is too near to our own territories for us not to be frequently incommoded by it. The only precaution to be observed in regard to these additional countries, would have been to form them into new kingdoms, declare them united with the rest of the Christian powers, and bestow them on different princes; carefully observing to exclude those who before bore rank among the sovereigns of Europe.

Maximilien de Béthune, Duke of Sully, *Memoirs* (1778).

Read the free English text online (1781 edition):
https://books.google.co.uk/books?id=9OI9AQAAMAAJ&lpg=P A313&dq=sully vervins memoirs&hl=fr&pg=PA66

Read the free text in the original language (1778 edition):
https://books.google.de/books?id=t-iAVIeyd8UC &printsec=frontcover

3. Europe: A Project for Peace

Political essayist Castel de Saint-Pierre (1658–1743),[i] *who was a member of the French Academy and a friend of Fontenelle, composed his* Project for Perpetual Peace in Europe *(1713) just as the belligerent parties of the War of Spanish Succession were negotiating the terms of peace that would culminate in the Treaties of Utrecht and Rastatt. He published the piece in 1713; it presented the most complete draft of his project to sustain lasting peace throughout the continent. He appealed for a federation of the states of Europe, sustained by the efficiency of a model of balance of power. He envisioned that the European sovereign states (France, Spain, England, Holland, Portugal, Switzerland, Florence, Genoa and its associates, the Papal States, Venice, Savoy, Lorraine, Denmark, the Holy Roman Emperor and Empire, Poland, Sweden, Muscovy) would sign a unifying treaty and hold a perennial congress in order to form one enduring society together. To resolve conflicts, a tribunal would sit in arbitration. This innovative composition earned him, alongside a certain celebrity, a reputation as a persistent believer in utopia. Having proposed to lay out the means of achieving lasting peace between the Christian states, he continues as follows:*

Thus I think it necessary to begin with a few reflections: first, on the need for the sovereigns of Europe, like any other men, to live in peaceful, unified, and everlasting society in order to find happiness; next, on the needs that bring them to have these wars between them, for either the possession or the partition of a few goods; lastly, I will consider the means they have employed thus far either to avoid war or to stand fast against war when it bears upon them.

I have found that these means are usually reduced to the exchange of mutual promises, found either in treaties of trade, truce, or peace, which specify territorial limits and other pretentions of reciprocity, or in agreements that offer guarantees or conceive offensive and permanent leagues that establish, maintain, or re-establish the balance of power of

---

i   https://commons.wikimedia.org/wiki/File:Castel-de-saintpierre02.jpg

mighty houses. This system has until now seemed the most prudent from which the sovereigns of Europe and their ministers have drawn their policies. [...]

1. The current constitution of Europe can never produce anything but almost perpetual War, because it can never ensure sufficient security for the enforcement of Treaties.

2. The balance of power between the House of France and the House of Austria will never ensure the security required to prevent either foreign Wars or civil Wars, and thus will never ensure the security required for either the conservation of the States or the conservation of Trade.

[...] I next tried to discover if the sovereigns could not then find enough security for the enforcement of mutual promises by establishing continuous arbitration between them. I found that if the eighteen main powers of Europe, in order to conserve the present governance, avoid internecine wars, and ensure the advantages of continual commerce from nation to nation, wanted to make a unifying treaty and hold a perennial congress—based on a similar model to that used by the seven sovereignties of Holland, the thirteen sovereignties of Switzerland,[ii] or the sovereignties of Germany—and form a European Union with the best parts of those unions (especially the German union, which composes more than two hundred powers), I found that, as I was saying, the weakest would have enough security that the most powerful of the great powers would be unable to harm them. Each would diligently keep mutual promises, commerce could continue uninterrupted, and all future conflicts would end through arbitration and without war. We will never come to such mutual safety without this. [...]

1. The same grounds and means that managed in the past to shape a permanent Society between the sovereignties of Germany are available to the Rulers of today, and could serve to form a permanent association of all the Christian sovereignties of Europe.

2. The endorsements that the majority of the Sovereigns of Europe gave to the project for a European Society proposed by Henry the

---

ii   The Republic of the Seven United Netherlands and the Confederacy of the Thirteen Canons were the usual designations for Holland and Switzerland at the time, and express the political organization of these states.

Great[iii] prove that there is hope that a similar Project would be approved by their successors.

[...] In its second draft, the project embraced all the States of the world; my friends pointed out that in the coming centuries most sovereigns of Asia and Africa will request a reception into the Union. This vision seemed so very distant, and encumbered with so many difficulties, that it overshadowed the whole project with an air, an appearance of impossibility that repelled every reader, with the result that some came to believe that even limited to a Christian Europe, the project would be impossible to achieve. I have thus found myself more willingly convinced of their perspective, that the European Union is enough for Europe, sufficient to conserve her perpetual peace, and will be powerful enough to preserve its borders and its trade despite those who would try to impede them. The general council that it could establish in the Indies might easily become the arbiter of sovereigns in that country, and by its authority prevent them from taking arms. The credit of the Union will consequently be so much greater amongst them that they know with certainty that it seeks only security for their commerce, and that trade will be nothing but advantageous to them, so that they will not think to attempt any kind of conquest, and they will see as enemies only the enemies of peace.

Charles-Irénée Castel de Saint-Pierre,
Project for Perpetual Peace in Europe (1713).

Read the free text in the original language (1713 edition, volume I):
http://gallica.bnf.fr/ark:/12148/bpt6k86492n?rk=21459;2

Read the free text in the original language (1713 edition, volume II):
http://gallica.bnf.fr/ark:/12148/bpt6k864930?rk=42918;4

---

iii   Henry IV of France, who is mentioned by Sully in the previous extract.

4. A Study of Abbé de Saint-Pierre's Suggestions

Jean-Jacques Rousseau (1712–1778),[i] who left fragments expressing his doubts regarding the feasibility of the Abbé de Saint-Pierre's reforms, also took copious notes on his Project for Perpetual Peace. *This summary version of his predecessor's ideas regarding a European confederation was what truly allowed them to circulate in Europe. At the beginning of his piece, to enter into his predecessor's views and uphold them, Rousseau uses history to develop some of the notions in new ways. Where Saint-Pierre mentions uniting sovereigns, Rousseau looks at uniting nations. His 'System of Europe' does not mean the plurality of European monarchies neutralising one another, but the interdependence of nations engendered by historical causes and whose relations are complex and ambivalent, since this European society was marked by unceasing wars.*

In addition to these formal Confederations, it is possible to frame others, less visible but none the less real, which are silently cemented by community of interests, by conformity of habits and customs, by the acceptance of common principles, by other ties which establish mutual relations between nations politically divided. Thus the Powers of Europe constitute a kind of whole, united by identity of religion, of moral standard, of international law; by letters, by commerce, and finally by a species of balance which is the inevitable result of all these ties and, however little any man may strive consciously to maintain it, is not to be destroyed so easily as many men imagine.

This concert of Europe has not always existed; and the special causes which produced it are still working to preserve it. The truth is that, before the conquests of the Romans, the nations of this continent, all sunk in barbarism and each utterly unknown to the others, had nothing

---

i   https://commons.wikimedia.org/wiki/File:Jean-Jacques_Rousseau_(painted_ portrait).jpg

in common beyond the character which belonged to them as men: a character which, degraded by the practice of slavery, differed little enough in their eyes from that which constitutes the brute. Accordingly the Greeks, vain and disputatious, divided mankind, it may almost be said, into two distinct races: the one—their own, of course—made to rule; the other—the entire rest of the world—created solely to be slaves. From this principle it followed that a Gaul or a Spaniard was no more to a Greek than a Kaffir or Red Indian; and the barbarians themselves were as deeply divided from each other as the Greeks from all of them.

But when these men, born to rule, had been conquered by their slaves the Romans, when half of the known universe had passed beneath the same yoke, a common bond of laws and government was established, and all found themselves members of the same empire. This bond was still further tightened by the recognised principle, either supremely wise or supremely foolish, of imparting to the conquered all the rights of the conqueror: above all, by the famous decree of Claudius, which placed all the subjects of Rome on the roll of her citizens.

Thus all members of the Empire were united in one body politic. They were further united by laws and civil institutions which reinforced the political bond by defining equitably, clearly and precisely, so far as this was possible in so vast an empire, the mutual rights and duties of the ruler and the subject, of one citizen as against another. The Code of Theodosius and the later legislation of Justinian constituted a new bond of justice and reason, which came in to replace the sovereign power at the very moment when it showed unmistakable signs of slackening. This did more than anything else to stave off the break-up of the Empire and to maintain its authority even over the barbarians who ravaged it.

A third and yet stronger bond was furnished by religion; and it cannot be denied that Europe, even now, is indebted more to Christianity than to any other influence for the union, however imperfect, which survives among her members. So true is this that the one nation which has refused to accept Christianity has always remained an alien among the rest. Christianity, so despised in its infancy, ended by serving as a sanctuary to its slanderers. And the Roman Empire, which had persecuted it for centuries with fruitless cruelty, drew from it a power which she could no longer find in her own strength. The missionaries did more for her than any victory; she despatched bishops to redeem the mistake of her generals and triumphed by the aid of the priest when her soldiers were defeated. It is thus that the Franks, the Goths, the Burgundians, the Lombards, the Avars and many others ended by recognising the authority of the Empire which they had mastered, by admitting, at least in appearance, not only the law of the Gospel, but also that of the Prince at whose command it had been preached to them.

Such was the respect which this august body inspired even in its death-throes that, to the very end, its conquerors felt themselves honoured by the acceptance of its titles. The very generals who had humbled the Empire became its ministers and officials; the proudest kings welcomed, nay even canvassed for, the patriciate, the prefecture, the consulate; and, like the lion who fawns upon the man he could easily devour, these terrible conquerors did homage to the imperial throne which they might at any moment have cast down.

Thus the priesthood and the Empire wove a bond between various nations which, without any real community of interests, of rights, or of mutual dependence, found a tie in common principles and beliefs, the influence of which still survives even after its foundation is withdrawn. The venerable phantom of the Roman Empire has never ceased to unite the nations which once formed part of it; and as, after the fall of the Empire, Rome still asserted her authority under another form,[ii] Europe, the home of the temporal and spiritual Powers, still retains a sense of fellowship far closer than is to be found elsewhere. The nations of the other continents are too scattered for mutual intercourse; and they lack any other point of union such as Europe has enjoyed.

There are other, and more special, causes for this difference. Europe is more evenly populated, more uniformly fertile; it is easier to pass from one part of her to another. The interests of her princes are united by ties of blood, by commerce, arts and colonies. Communication is made easy by countless rivers winding from one country to another. An inbred love of change impels her inhabitants to constant travel, which frequently leads them to foreign lands. The invention of printing and the

---

ii   Respect for the Roman Empire has so completely survived her power that many jurists have questioned whether the Emperor of Germany is not the natural sovereign of the world; and Bartholus carried this doctrine so far as to treat anyone who dared to deny it as a heretic. The writings of the canonists are full of the corresponding doctrine of the temporal supremacy of the Roman Church [author's note].

general love of letters has given them a basis of common knowledge and common intellectual pursuits. Finally, the number and smallness of her States, the cravings of luxury and the large diversity of climates which Europe offers for their satisfaction, make them all necessary to each other. All these causes combine to make of Europe not, like Asia and Africa, a purely imaginary assemblage of peoples with nothing in common save the name, but a real community with a religion and a moral code, with customs and even laws of its own, which none of the component nations can renounce without causing a shock to the whole frame.

Now look at the other side of the picture. Observe the perpetual quarrels, the robberies, the usurpations, the revolts, the wars, the murders, which bring daily desolation to this venerable home of philosophy, this brilliant sanctuary of art and science. Consider our fair speeches and our abominable acts, the boundless humanity of our maxims and the boundless cruelty of our deeds; our religion so merciful and our intolerance so ferocious; our policy so mild in our text-books and so harsh in our acts; our rulers so beneficent and our people so wretched; our Governments so temperate and our wars so savage: and then tell me how to reconcile these glaring contradictions; tell me if this alleged brotherhood of the nations of Europe is anything more than a bitter irony to denote their mutual hatred.

But, in truth, what else was to be expected? Every community without laws and without rulers, every union formed and maintained by nothing better than chance, must inevitably fall into quarrels and dissensions at the first change that comes about. The historic union of the nations of Europe has entangled their rights and interests in a thousand complications; they touch each other at so many points that no one of them can move without giving a jar to all the rest; their variances are all the more deadly, as their ties are more closely woven; their frequent quarrels are almost as savage as civil wars.

Let us admit then that the Powers of Europe stand to each other strictly in a state of war, and that all the separate treaties between them are in the nature rather of a temporary truce than a real peace: whether because such treaties are seldom guaranteed by any except the contracting parties; or because the respective rights of those parties are never thoroughly determined and are therefore bound — they, or the claims which pass for rights in the eyes of the Powers who recognise no earthly superior—to give rise to fresh wars as soon as a change of circumstances shall have given fresh strength to the claimants. [...]

The causes of the disease, once known, suffice to indicate the remedy, if indeed there is one to be found. Everyone can see that what unites any form of society is community of interests, and what disintegrates is their conflict; that either tendency may be changed or modified by a thousand accidents; and therefore that, as soon as a society is founded, some coercive power must be provided to co-ordinate the actions of its members and give to their common interests and mutual obligations that firmness and consistency which they could never acquire of themselves.

It would, indeed, be a great mistake to suppose that the reign of violence, described above, could ever be remedied by the mere force of circumstances, or without the aid of human wisdom. The present balance of Europe is just firm enough to remain in perpetual oscillation without losing itself altogether; and, if our troubles cannot increase, still less can we put an end to them, seeing that any sweeping revolution is henceforth an impossibility.

Jean-Jacques Rousseau,
A Lasting Peace Through the Federation of Europe (1761).

Read the free English text online (1917 edition):
http://lf-oll.s3.amazonaws.com/titles/1010/0147_Bk.pdf

Read the free text in the original language (1826 edition):
http://gallica.bnf.fr/ark:/12148/bpt6k2051816

5. Universal Peace

Influenced by Saint-Pierre and his Project for Peace, the German philosopher Immanuel Kant (1724–1804)[i] published his own treatise Zum ewigen Frieden. Ein philosophischer Entwurf (Perpetual Peace: A Philosophical Sketch) *in 1795. The text rapidly circulated throughout Europe. Kant moved on from the idea of perpetual peace in Europe and came up with the idea of universal peace, to be founded on liberty, equality, fraternity and reason. Unlike Saint-Pierre, he does not go into the minutiae of his plan. His reflections relate more generally to the philosophy of law.*

Article II: No State that exists for itself (whether small or large) shall be acquirable by another through inheritance, exchange, purchase, or donation.

For a State (as compared, for example, to the ground on which it has its seat) is not a property (*patrimonium*). It is a society of human beings, over whom no one else but itself may rule and dispose. But to incorporate such a State, which is itself a trunk with its own roots, as a graft into another State, means to abolish its existence as a moral person, and to make of the latter a thing, and therefore contradicts the idea of the original contract, without which no right over a people is conceivable. The danger that the prejudiced preference for this mode of acquisition has, up to our own times, brought to Europe, for it was never known in the other parts of the world, is well known to everybody, namely that States could also marry one another, partly as a new kind of industry by which one could make oneself all powerful without expense of effort through family alliances, partly also to expand one's landed property. [...]

Second definitive article on perpetual peace. The law of nations shall be founded upon a federalism of free States.

Peoples, as States, can be viewed like individual human beings, who, in their natural state (i.e. independent from external laws) already injure

---

i   https://commons.wikimedia.org/wiki/File:Kant_foto.jpg

one another through their coexistence, and of whom everyone, for the sake of their safety, can and should demand of others to enter into a constitution similar to that of civil society, in which everyone's right can be secured. That would be a confederation of peoples, which would not however need be a nation State. [...]

But since reason, from the throne of the highest moral legislative power, absolutely condemns war as a course of law and, on the contrary, makes the state of peace an immediate duty, which cannot, however, be achieved or secured without a treaty among peoples—therefore there must be a federation of a particular kind, which one could call the federation of peace (*foedus pacificum*), which would differ from the peace treaty (*pactum pacis*) in the sense that the latter seeks to end merely one war, the former however seeks to end all wars forever.

The practicability (objective reality) of this idea of federalism, which should eventually encompass all States, and thereby lead to perpetual peace, can be demonstrated. For if luck would have it that a powerful and enlightened people were to form themselves into a republic (which must be inclined toward perpetual peace by its very nature), then this would offer a centre for the federal union of other States to join and thereby to secure the freedom of all participating States in accordance with the idea of the law of nations, and, through multiple bonds of this kind, gradually spread ever further in the course of time. [...]

Third definitive article on perpetual peace. The right of world citizenship shall be restricted to the conditions of universal hospitality.

Here, as in the preceding articles, we are speaking not of philanthropy, but of law, and there hospitality (the quality of being a host) means the right of a foreigner not to be treated with hostility by another upon arriving on that other's soil. The foreigner can be refused, if this can occur without their destruction; so long, however, as the foreigner behaves peacefully wherever they reside, they may not be treated with hostility. [...]

In this way distant parts of the world can enter into peaceful relations with each other, which finally become publicly lawful, and can thereby bring the human race ever closer to a world-wide constitution. [...]

If one compares this to the inhospitable conduct of the civilized, primarily mercantile states of our part of the world, the injustice they commit when visiting foreign countries and peoples (which they consider one and the same upon conquest) reaches the point of horror. […]

Supplement. Of the guarantee of perpetual peace.

She [Nature] employs two means to prevent peoples from intermixing and to separate them from each other: the difference of languages and religions. These carry with them the tendency towards mutual hatred and the pretext for war, but, with growing culture and increasing closeness of the peoples the diversity of tongues and faiths, leads to greater unity in principles, to agreement in a peace that is brought forth and secured not through the weakening of all powers, as in despotism (on the graveyard of freedom), but through their balance, through their most vigorous competition. […]

It is the spirit of trade that cannot coexist with war, and that sooner or later possesses every people.

Immanuel Kant, *Perpetual Peace: A Philosophical Sketch* (1796).

Read the text in the original language (2014 edition):
http://www.gutenberg.org/files/46873/46873-h/46873-h.htm

6. What Size Should Europe Be?

In his Project for Perpetual Peace in Europe,[i] *Charles-Irénée Castel de Saint-Pierre proposes the association of neighbouring Islamic states with the European Union by treaty, in order to ensure long-term settlement with them; the successive and unsuccessful truces of the past should give way to a new paradigm.*

With respect to the Mahomeddans neighbouring Europe, the Tartars, the Turks, the Tunisians, Tripolitans,[ii] the Algerians and Moroccans, I have been told that it would hardly be within the bounds of propriety to give them a voice in the Congress: might they even refuse to accept? Nevertheless, the Union, in order to maintain peace and trade with them, and avoid constant defence against them, could form a treaty with them to ensure all the same securities and accord them each representation

---

i   https://commons.wikimedia.org/wiki/File:Saint-Pierre_-_Projet_pour_rendre_la_
     paix_perpétuelle_en_Europe_-_Tome_1,_1713.djvu
ii   Read: Libyans (from Tripoli).

in the city of peace. If they turn down such a treaty, the Union could then declare them as enemies, and compel them by force to provide the security required for the conventions of peace. It would also be easy to obtain several articles in favour of their Christian subjects.

Charles-Irénée Castel de Saint-Pierre,
Project for Perpetual Peace in Europe (1713).

**Read the free text in the original language
(1713 edition, volume I):**
http://gallica.bnf.fr/ark:/12148/bpt6k86492n?rk=21459;2

**Read the free text in the original language
(1713 edition, volume II):**
http://gallica.bnf.fr/ark:/12148/bpt6k864930?rk=42918;4

7. The European Union: An Unrealistic Project?

In his Judgment on Perpetual Peace, *Jean-Jacques Rousseau expresses his reservations regarding the realisation of an enterprise like Saint-Pierre's. He sees the main obstacle as the egoism of sovereigns. He recognizes that the late Abbé's reflections were of irrefutable importance and worthy of occupying a good man.*

If ever any moral truth has been demonstrated, it seems to me to be the general and particular usefulness of this Project. The advantages which would come from its realisation for each Prince, each People and for all of Europe are immense, clear, incontestable; there is nothing more solid nor more exact than the reasoning the author uses to establish this: to create his European Republic for a day would be enough to make it last eternally, so readily would each person see from his or her own experience the individual gain in the common good. However the same princes who would defend it with all their strength if it existed, would oppose its realisation now with equal strength, and will unfailingly prevent its establishment, just as they would prevent its expiration. Thus the work of the Abbé de Saint-Pierre on perpetual peace appears at first useless for producing it and superfluous for preserving it. It is then simply vain speculation, some impatient reader will say; no, it is a solid and sensible book; it is very important that it exists.

Let us begin by examining the objections of those who do not judge reasons by reason but only by the event, and who have nothing to say against this project, except that it has not been carried out. In fact, they will say, if these advantages are so significant, why then have the Sovereigns of Europe not adopted it? Why do they neglect their own interests, if those interests have been so well demonstrated?

Doubtless, that is plausible, at least if one supposes their wisdom to be equal to their ambition, and that they see their advantage all the better for desiring it more strongly, when in fact the great punishment of an excess of pride is always to employ means which injure it, and the very heat of the passions is almost always what diverts them from their goal. Let us then distinguish in politics as in morals between true interests and apparent interests: the first would be found in perpetual peace, that is shown in the project. The second is found in the state of absolute independence which shields the Sovereigns from a mad Pilot. To display a vain knowledge and to give orders to his sailors, he would prefer to drift between rocks during the storm rather than enslave his vessel with anchors.

All the business of Kings, or of those to whom they grant their powers, concerns two goals: extending their domination without and increasing its scope within; any other way of looking at things either concerns one of these two goals or simply serves as a pretext for them; as, for example, the public good, the happiness of the subjects, and the glory of the nation, words forever banished from the cabinet and so weightily employed in public edicts, that they are only ever harbingers of gloomy orders, and the people groan in advance when their masters speak to them of their fatherly care. [...]

One must not believe either, as the Abbé de Saint-Pierre does, that even with the good will that neither the Princes nor the Ministers will ever have, it would be easy to find a moment favourable to the implementation of this system. For this, it would be necessary for the sum of individual interests not to be more important than the common interest, and for each person to believe he or she saw in the good of all the greatest good one could hope for oneself. This, however, requires wisdom to come together in so many minds and relationships to come together in so many interests that one must not hope that the chance harmony of all the necessary circumstances will arise from luck alone; however if this harmony has not arrived, it is only force which can replace it, and then it is no longer a question of persuasion but rather of compulsion, and one must not write books, but raise armies.

Jean-Jacques Rousseau, *Judgment on Perpetual Peace* (1756–1758).

Read the free text in the original language (1826 edition):
http://gallica.bnf.fr/ark:/12148/bpt6k2051816

8. Judgment on Perpetual Peace

Few historians can claim to have had an influence as durable as Englishman Edward Gibbon (1737–1794)[i] with his Decline and Fall of the Roman Empire *(1776), a study which shows its reader a retrospective panorama, but includes elements that allow us to envisage the future more serenely.*

It is the duty of a patriot to prefer and promote the exclusive interest and glory of his native country; but a philosopher may be permitted to enlarge his views, and to consider Europe as one great republic, whose various inhabitants have attained almost the same level of politeness and cultivation. The balance of power will continue to fluctuate and the prosperity of our own, or the neighbouring kingdoms, may be alternately exalted or depressed; but these partial events cannot essentially injure our general state of happiness, the system of arts, and laws, and manners.

Edward Gibbon,
The History of the Decline and Fall of the Roman Empire (1776–1788).

Read the free English text online (1997 edition):
https://www.gutenberg.org/files/25717/25717-h/25717-h.htm

---

i   https://commons.wikimedia.org/wiki/File:Edward_Gibbon_by_Henry_Walton_cleaned.jpg

9. Europe in the *Encyclopédie*

In the French Encyclopédie ou Dictionnaire raisonné des sciences, des arts et des métiers *coordinated by Diderot and D'Alembert, known throughout Europe simply as the* Encyclopédie, *and one of the most influential works of the European Enlightenment, Louis de Jaucourt (1704–1779),[i] author of hundreds of articles, provides a geographical description of Europe as one of the globe's four continents – Australasia not yet at that point being known to the western world – and describes its rich cultural heritage.*

EUROPE, (*Geog*[*raphy*]) great region of the inhabited world. Perhaps the most plausible etymology of the word *Europe* is a derivation from the Phoenician *urappa*, which in that tongue signifies *white face*; an epithet that could have no doubt been given to the daughter of Agenor, sister of Cadmus, but which at any rate suits Europeans, themselves being neither brown-skinned like southern Asians, nor black like Africans.

Europe has not always had the same name, nor indeed the same divisions between the main peoples who have occupied it; and as far as the subdivisions are concerned, they depend on a level of detail impossible to reconstruct, for want of historians who would be able to guide us out of this labyrinth.

In this article, however, instead of considering Europe as the ancients knew it, where their writings have even come down to us, I wish only to comment briefly here on its boundaries.

At its widest point, Europe extends from Cape St Vincent in Portugal and the Algarve on the Atlantic coast, to the mouth of the Ob river in the Northern Ocean, covering a distance of 1200 French leagues of 20 to a degree, or 900 German miles. Its greatest length, measured from Cape Matapan, in the south of Morea to the North Cape in the northernmost point of Norway, is approximately 733 French leagues of 20 to a degree,

---

i   https://commons.wikimedia.org/wiki/File:ChevalierLouisJaucourt.jpg

or 550 German miles. It is bordered in the east by Asia, in the south by Africa, from which it is separated by the Mediterranean Sea, in the west by the Atlantic or Western Ocean, and to the north by the Frozen sea.

Reason and Philosophy, the one lifting and the other tearing off Truth's veil. Frontispiece of the *Encyclopédie, ou Dictionnaire raisonné des sciences, des arts et des métiers.*[ii]

I do not know whether we are right to divide the world into four parts of which Europe is one, not least because such a division is inexact in that it excludes the Arctic and Antarctic territories, which despite being lesser-known, nevertheless exist and deserve their blank space on globes and maps.

In any case, Europe remains the smallest part of the world. However, as the author of *The Spirit of the Laws* [Montesquieu] notes, it has achieved such a high degree of power that history has scarcely anything to compare it to, if we consider the immensity of its expenditure, the extent

---

ii   https://commons.wikimedia.org/wiki/File:Encyclopedie_frontispice_section_
      256px.jpg

of its commitments, the size of its armed forces, what is required for their upkeep, even when they are mostly useless and only kept for show.

Besides, it matters little that *Europe* is the smallest of these four parts of the world by area, for it is the greatest of all in its trade, its exploration, its agricultural yield, in its enlightenment and the industriousness of its peoples, in its knowledge of the Arts, the Sciences and Trades, and most importantly of all, in its Christianity, whose beneficent moral teachings bring nothing but happiness to society. It is thanks to this religion that our government recognises a certain political right, and that in war people are protected by a sort of right, something for which human nature can never be sufficiently grateful; in appearing to have as its sole objective happiness in another life, it provides happiness in this one too. Europe was called 'Celtic' in the most ancient of days. It lies geographically between 9 and 93 degrees longitude, and between 34 and 74 degrees latitude. The *Geographers* will supply the reader with further information.

Louis de Jaucourt, 'Europe',
in the *Encyclopédie* of Diderot and D'Alembert (1756).

Read the free text in the original language (1756 edition):
https://fr.wikisource.org/wiki/L'Encyclopédie/1re_édition/
Volume_6

10. The Geography of Europe

Diego de Torres Villarroel (1693–1770),[i] who was a professor at the University of Salamanca, a mathematician, a priest and a dramatist, wrote The Fantastic Voyage of the Great Piscátor of Salamanca (1724), *which gives a geographical description of Europe that reminds us of the limits of knowledge at a time when the very existence of Australasia was unknown in Europe.*

It is clear from the circumnavigations of the globe that it is divided into two continents or main areas of land. The first comprises the entire area of the Arctic Pole and the four main regions of the world: Europe, Asia, Africa and America and the other part or continent includes the entire unknown territory to the South and these two areas or continents are separated by the Ocean. The continent that encompasses the southern territory remains unknown […]. Europe extends one thousand and fifty leagues from East to West and spans seven hundred and forty-nine leagues from North to South. To the North it borders on the frozen sea, to the West on the Atlantic Sea, to the South on the Strait of Gibraltar and to the East on the Ægean sea. Apart from its islands, its fourteen largest and most important provinces are: Spain, France, Italy, Germany, The Netherlands, Poland, Hungary, Illyricum, Romania, Bulgaria, Serbia, Lesser Tartary, The Grand Duchy of Moscow, Moldova, Walachia and Scandinavia.

Diego de Torres Villarroel,
The Fantastic Voyage of the Great Piscátor of Salamanca (1724).

Read the free text in the original language:
http://biblioteca.org.ar/libros/132245.pdf

---

i   https://commons.wikimedia.org/wiki/File:Diego_de_Torres_Villarroel.jpg

11. History and Political Interests

Since Pierre Bayle at the end of the seventeenth century, lexicographers have often slipped subversive truths into seemingly innocuous encyclopaedia entries. This article titled 'Academy of History' is no exception, since it tackles the question of how history is written and denounces the insidious suppression of the truth in various western nations.

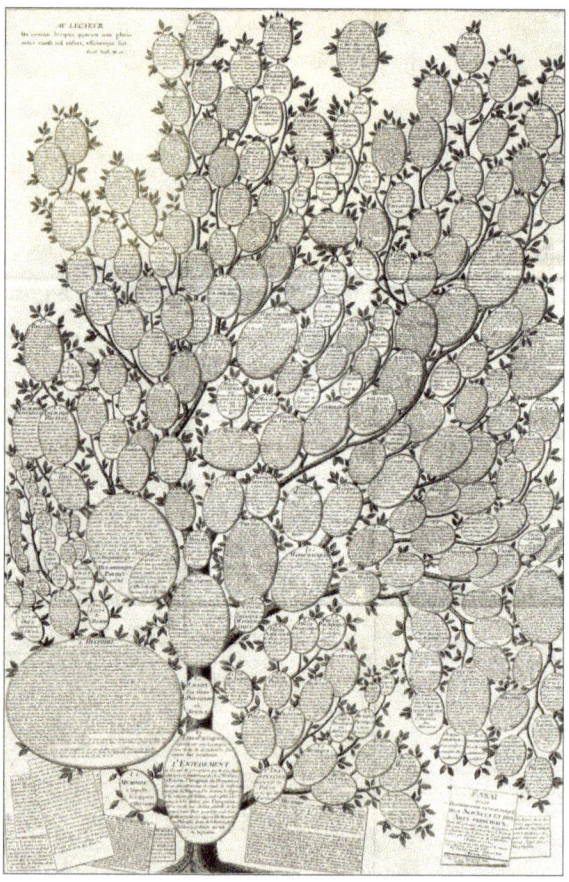

Figurative system showing the arborescence of human knowledge in the *Supplément à l'Encyclopédie* (1776), engraved by Robert Bénard.[i]

---

i   https://commons.wikimedia.org/wiki/File:Encyclopédie-_Diderot's_Tree_of_ Knowledge.tif

No country, no prince has yet thought to found an academy of history, whose principal aim would be to observe the different states of the nation carefully, to transmit events to posterity with the most sincere truth, and to perfect the science of morality and legislation, whose sole bases are historical facts, just as natural phenomena are the sole basis of physics. But knowledge of the former is all the more useful, since it matters a great deal more to a State to know which are the best laws to banish laziness and to inspire in its citizens a love of their country and of virtue, than to know what laws observe the movements of the four different satellites of Jupiter. Why then abandon the writing of history, which we are right to call the eye of the future, as well as that of the past, and the torch of life? Why not follow the example of the Chinese, who have excelled so strongly in morality and in legislation? They have founded a tribunal of history in which they keep a register of all that happens under the reign of each emperor with the same exactitude as we note in our academies the appulsions[ii] of the moon to the stars, the eclipses and all that occurs in the Heavens. After the death of the emperor, the record is divulged to serve to instruct his successors, and as a guide for public happiness. In several European States, there are offices for historiographers, and public chairs of history. That is a start towards the academy of history that we propose, it would be easy to extend these beginnings and to form from them a fixed establishment from which we might draw great benefits for the good administration of the States and the happiness of the people, which must always be the supreme law.

We must observe, however, that knowledge of moral causes does not demand as much wisdom as does knowledge of natural causes. Perhaps Europe has no need of the former, of an academy of *savants*, or a tribunal of mandarins, necessary for China, where the human spirit seems to be less active. Moreover, the dose of liberty, which can be found in several European governments, naturally moves all men to seek out the true causes of historical facts, and to publish them; which may be done without danger, in England above all, where they still enjoy happy times as the Romans had under Trajan. Whereas in China,

---

ii   This scientific term, which was not lexicalized at the time, and which is calqued on the Latin, denotes the convergence of celestial bodies found in conjunction with one another, but without an occultation or eclipse occurring.

where despotism has raised its throne, no-one would dare to speak the language of truth, if, in the interest of the public good, the government had not accorded this privilege to a tribunal before which the emperors are summoned after their death. Thus what appears at first glance to be in China the pinnacle to which legislation might be taken, is perhaps only its correction. That may be so, but have we no need of this correction in several of our European governments, where the truth is too often held captive, and where indistinct and hidden despotism is all the more arbitrary, whereas that of China is truly a legal despotism.

'Academy of History',
in *Supplement to the Encyclopédie* (1776).

Read the free text in the original language (1776 edition):
http://gallica.bnf.fr/ark:/12148/bpt6k50550x/f1.image

12. A Prototype for the European Parliament?

According to Sully,[i] the King of France had imagined, amongst the institutions necessary to govern the associated states, that there should be a 'general Council of Europe' entrusted with managing several aspects of the Union.

The model of this general council of Europe had been formed on that of the ancient Amphictyons[ii] of Greece, with such alterations only as rendered it suitable to our customs, climate and policy. It consisted of a certain number of commissaries, ministers, or plenipotentiaries from all the governments of the Christian republic, who were to be constantly assembled as a senate, to deliberate on any affairs which might occur; to discuss the different interests, pacify the quarrels, clear up and determine all the civil, political, and religious affairs of Europe, whether within itself or with its neighbours. The form and manner of proceeding in the senate would have been more particularly determined by the suffrages of the senate itself. Henry was of opinion that it should be composed of four commissaries from each of the following potentates: The Emperor, the Pope, the kings of France, Spain, England, Denmark, Sweden, Lombardy, Poland, and the republic of Venice; and of two only from the other republics and inferior powers, which all together would

---

i   https://commons.wikimedia.org/wiki/File:Charles-Irenée-Castel-de-Saint-Pierre-Projet-de-traité-pour-rendre-la-paix_MG_0660.tif

ii   In Delphi, the council of the Amphictyons handled public affairs.

have composed a senate of about sixty-six persons, who should have been re-chosen every three years.

Maximilien de Béthune, Duke of Sully, *Memoirs* (1778).

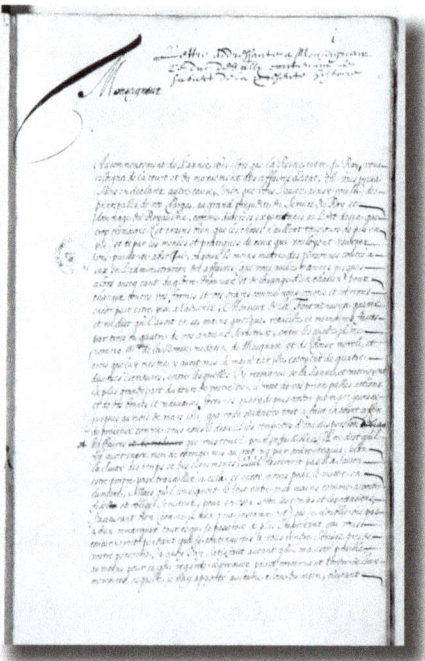

Maximilien de Béthune, Duke of Sully, *Memoirs*
(manuscript of the first volume).[iii]

Read the free English text online (1781 edition):
https://books.google.co.uk/books?id=9OI9AQAAMAAJ&lpg=P
A313&dq=sully vervins memoirs&hl=fr&pg=PA89

Read the free text in the original language (1778 edition):
https://books.google.de/books?id=t-iAVIeyd8UC
&printsec=frontcover

---

iii   http://gallica.bnf.fr/ark:/12148/btv1b9007257z/f6.item

13. Europe and Islam

When discussing the relationship between European nations (which he defines as Christian) and Muslim countries, Charles-Irénée Castel de Saint-Pierre betrays a eurocentrism founded on a conception of a Europe unified by a Christian faith.

It is widely known that the primary reason Muslim sovereigns do not establish colleges and distance their subjects from the study of science and fine arts is a fear of the schisms and wars often caused by the disputes of theologians. Until now they have believed that only broad ignorance can protect them from this affliction; but as soon as they see that in association with the European Society they will have the assurance of the conservation of peace both within and without their borders, it is likely that they would soon adopt methods used by Christian states for the education of youth and the advancement of the arts and sciences. Thus, this could represent for them a new motivation to do everything in their power to found and confirm this grand establishment. The Church would benefit, in that the more Mahommedans become enlightened, the less they will remain attached to their dogmas, and the more they will be disposed to understand the beauty and perfection of the Christian faith.

Charles-Irénée Castel de Saint-Pierre,
Project for Perpetual Peace in Europe (1713).

**Read the free text in the original language
(1713 edition, volume I):**
http://gallica.bnf.fr/ark:/12148/bpt6k86492n?rk=21459;2

**Read the free text in the original language
(1713 edition, volume II):**
http://gallica.bnf.fr/ark:/12148/bpt6k864930?rk=42918;4

14. Europe's True Wealth is its Cultural Heritage

In his 1756 historiographical Essai sur les mœurs et l'esprit des nations *(Essay on the Mores and the Spirit of the Nations), Voltaire (1694–1778)[i] stresses the wealth of the cultural inheritance of the continent, which he describes as a part of a world 'incomparably more populated, more civilised, richer and more enlightened' than it was during the Roman Empire, even though Italy alone has lost some of its radiance. He mentions the fear he shares with other contemporary thinkers like Montesquieu that the world's population might be decreasing, and criticizes clerical celibacy, which he considered to be an aberration.*

Let one consider, from Petersburg to Madrid, the prodigious number of superb towns built on sites which were deserts six hundred years ago; let one pay attention to the immense forests which covered the earth from the banks of the Danube to the Baltic sea, and even to the middle of France. It is quite obvious that when many lands have been reclaimed, there are many men. Whatever one might say, agriculture and commerce are more widespread than they were previously. [...]

In what a flourishing state Europe would be without the continuous wars which trouble it for very minor interests and often for tiny whims! How high a degree of perfection might the farming of land not have reached, and how much more succour and comfort the manufacturing arts might have spread in civil life, if such a surprising number of useless men and women had not been entombed in monasteries! A new humanity which has been introduced into the scourge of war and which softens its horrors helped contribute to saving people from a destruction which appears to threaten them at all times. The multitude of soldiers continually maintained by all princes is, in truth, a quite deplorable

---

i   https://commons.wikimedia.org/wiki/File:Atelier_de_Nicolas_de_Largillière,_portrait_de_Voltaire,_détail_(musée_Carnavalet)_-002.jpg

evil. And yet, as has already been remarked, this evil produces good: people no longer take part in the war their masters wage; citizens of besieged towns often pass from one domination to another, without a single inhabitant having lost his or her life: they are simply the prize for he who had the most soldiers, canons and money.

Civil wars long brought desolation to Germany, England, France; but such distress was soon repaired and the flourishing state of these lands proves that the industry of men has gone much farther than their fury. The same is not true of Persia, for instance, which has fallen prey to devastations for the past forty years; but if it unites under a wise prince, it will regain its solidity in less time than it took to lose it. [...]

When a nation knows the arts, when it is not subjugated and transported by foreigners, it can easily emerge from its ruins and it always recovers.

Voltaire, *Essay on the Mores and the Spirit of Nations* (1756).

Read the free text in the original language (1829 edition):
http://gallica.bnf.fr/ark:/12148/bpt6k375239

15. Making Rules to Bring about Peace

Like many other intellectuals of his time, Condorcet (1743–1794)[i] believed that the Reformation helped bring about an improvement in the state of Europe. He was one of the defenders of perfectibility and thus considered that, as had happened after other historic periods of upheaval, progress should ultimately lead to positive changes.

Concerned with the common interests which united them, and the opposing interests they believed they had, the nations of Europe felt the need to recognise certain rules amongst themselves, to preside over their pacific ties, independently from treaties; even in the midst of war, other rules, being duly respected, would soften its outrages, diminish is ravages and, at the very least, prevent useless evils.

Marie-Jean-Antoine-Nicolas de Caritat, Marquis de Condorcet, *Outlines of an Historical View of the Progress of the Human Mind* (1794).

Read the free English text online (1795 edition):
https://books.google.co.uk/books?id=SLs8AAAAYAAJ&dq=co
ndorcet america africa asia&pg=PA188

Read the free text in the original language (1822 edition):
https://books.google.de/books?id=hRIPAAAAQAAJ
&printsec=frontcover

---

i   https://commons.wikimedia.org/wiki/File:Nicolas_de_Condorcet.PNG

16. Our Russian Neighbour

If he accounts for relations with neighbouring Muslim countries, Saint-Pierre in his Project for Perpetual Peace in Europe *also considers the interests of the Tsar and thus of Russia. He demonstrates the role that potential exchanges could play in the consolidation of equilibrium on the continent.*

The Tsar has demonstrated his passion for encouraging the growth of commerce in the provinces. In this, he has significant advantages from nature, as great rivers span his country and he has ports on the Ocean, the Baltic Sea, and the Caspian Sea. The territory is extremely fertile in abundant areas, the population is numerous; achievement of perfection in manufacturing and the arts lacks only frequent and perpetual exchange with the best regulated nations. Moreover, he has recently discovered from experience how much war retards the accomplishment of those fine projects he has achieved in those areas; thus, it seems likely that once he becomes aware of a project that will bring perpetual peace among Christians, he will eagerly seek any method that will help it succeed.

Charles-Irénée Castel de Saint-Pierre,
Project for Perpetual Peace in Europe (1713).

**Read the free text in the original language
(1713 edition, volume I):**
http://gallica.bnf.fr/ark:/12148/bpt6k86492n?rk=21459;2

**Read the free text in the original language
(1713 edition, volume II):**
http://gallica.bnf.fr/ark:/12148/bpt6k864930?rk=42918;4

17. Christian Europe as a Great Republic?

In Chapter Two, 'On the States of Europe before Louis XIV', of his historiographical treatise The Century of Louis XIV, *Voltaire (1694–1778) underlines the common legal principles of Christian Europe before Louis XIV came to the French throne.*

For a long time, Christian Europe (with the exception of Russia) could have been viewed as a sort of large republic split into several States, some of which were monarchies, others mixed; some aristocratic, others popular; but all corresponding with each other; all having a same basis of religion, though they were divided into several sects; all having the same principles of public law and politics, unknown in the other parts of the world. It is thanks to such principles that European nations do not make their prisoners into slaves, respect the ambassadors of their enemies, agree together about the pre-eminence and particular rights of certain Princes, like the Emperor, Kings and other lesser potentates; and that they agree above all on the wise policy of trying inasmuch as possible to maintain amongst themselves an equal balance of power, always employing negotiations, even in the middle of war, and maintaining, in each other's lands, ambassadors or less honourable spies capable of warning all the courts of a single one's plans, at once to sound the alarm in Europe and to secure the weakest against the invasions the strongest is always ready to undertake.

Voltaire, *The Century of Louis XIV* (1751).

Read the free text in the original language (1878 edition):
https://fr.wikisource.org/wiki/Le_Siècle_de_Louis_XIV

18. Unity in Diversity?

In his treatise Paris, the Model of Foreign Nations, or French Europe *(1777[i]), Louis-Antoine Caraccioli (1719–1803), polymath and author of philosophical, historical and religious works, presents a sweeping panorama of Europe in the latter half of the eighteenth century, a Europe dominated by the influence of French culture.*

On different Nations

God forbid that I should use this treatise to belittle the Europeans so as to exalt the French.

Be you Italian, English, Spanish, Russian, Swedish, Portuguese etc. you are all my brothers, all my friends, all equally courageous and virtuous. Fortunate is he who, as a citizen of the world, knows neither antipathy nor prejudice.

---

i   http://gallica.bnf.fr/ark:/12148/bpt6k1156961

If I separate you into different groups, it is only because you have different ways of living, for as nature has forged no two beings entirely the same, neither has she formed any two peoples with the same mixture of steadiness and volatility. The world truly is a bouquet of flowers, wherein the Frenchman is as colourful as a carnation, the Italian dazzles like a rose, the Englishman glowers sombre as the thoughtful pansy, etc. They do all form the most striking contrast.

Neither are territory or climate the only things which differentiate nations, the only thing which chills the Dutch or sets the Italian ablaze. Their form of government profoundly influences both spirit and customs. We do not see the same behaviour or ideas in a despotic country as in a republican State. The Englishman sees things close up, whereas the Muslim sees them as if from afar. It's the same as with a telescope, where one end makes things look smaller while the other makes them look bigger.

Be this as it may, there has always been a dominant nation which all others try to imitate. In times gone by everything was Roman, and now everything is French. These changes happen with the centuries. There is nothing beneath the stars, themselves continually revolving, which is not also variable, and on Earth this is particularly so, the human mind being naturally restless, proud of continuous change, and taking pleasure in trying out new things.

Louis-Antoine Caraccioli,
Paris, the Model of Foreign Nations, or French Europe (1777).

Read the free text in the original language (1777 edition):
http://gallica.bnf.fr/ark:/12148/bpt6k1156961

🔊 **Listen to the free audio book in the original language:**
http://gallica.bnf.fr/ark:/12148/bpt6k1156961/f3.vocal

19. European Commerce

In The Spirit of Laws (1748) *Montesquieu (1689–1755)[i] includes a history of commerce in Book Twenty-One in order to measure the effects of the 'revolutions' by which it is affected. The world's new geopolitical situation differs from what the 'histories of all the nations' can offer. That is why its own history must be retraced. Europe is the pivot of worldwide exchanges, but is not an unchanging centre. Far from leading to simple eurocentrism, the consideration of the multiple and complex relations born of trade's revolution are an invitation to renew our investigation of the links between politics and economics, and they put strain on certain ideas regarding commercial exchanges.*

It is still a fundamental law of Europe, that all commerce with a foreign colony shall be regarded as a mere monopoly, punishable by the laws of the country; and in this case we are not to be directed by the laws and precedents of the Ancients, which are not at all applicable.

It is likewise acknowledged, that a commerce established between the mother countries does not include a permission to trade in the colonies; for these always continue in a state of prohibition.

The disadvantage of a colony that loses the liberty of commerce, is visibly compensated by the protection of the mother country, who defends it by her arms, or supports it by her laws.

From hence follows a third law of Europe, that when a foreign commerce with a colony is prohibited, it is not lawful to trade in those seas, except in such cases as are excepted by treaty.

Nations who are with respect to the whole universe what individuals are in a State, like these, are governed by the law of nature, and by the particular laws of their own making. One nation may resign to another

---

i   https://commons.wikimedia.org/wiki/File:Montesquieu_1.png

the sea as well as the land. The Carthaginians forbade the Romans to sail beyond certain limits, as the Greeks had obliged the King of Persia to keep as far distant from the sea coast as a horse could gallop.

The great distance of our colonies is not an inconvenience that affects their safety; for if the mother country, on whom they depend for their defence, is far distant, no less distant are those nations by whom they may be afraid of being conquered.

Besides, this distance is the cause that those who are established there, cannot conform to the manner of living in a climate so different from their own; they are obliged therefore to draw from the mother country all the conveniences of life. The Carthaginians, to render the Sardinians and Corsicans more dependent, forbade their planting, sowing, or doing anything of the like kind under pain of death; so that they supplied them with necessaries from Africa. The Europeans have compassed the same thing, without having recourse to such severe laws. Our colonies in the Caribbean islands are under an admirable regulation in this respect; the subject of their commerce is what we neither have nor can produce and they want what is the subject of ours.

A consequence of the discovery of America was, the connecting Asia and Africa with Europe; it furnished materials for a trade with that vast part of Asia, known by the name of the East Indies. Silver, that metal so useful as the medium of commerce, became now as a merchandise, the basis of the greatest commerce in the world. *In fine*, the navigation to Africa became necessary, in order to furnish us with men to labour in the mines, and to cultivate the lands of America.

Europe is arrived to so high a degree of power, that nothing in history can be compared to it; whether we consider the immensity of its expenses, the grandeur of its engagements, the number of its troops, and the regular payment even of those that are least serviceable, and which are kept only for ostentation.

Father Du Halde[ii] says, that the interior trade of China is much greater than that of all Europe. That might be, if our foreign trade did not augment our inland commerce. Europe carries on the trade and

---

ii   The French Jesuit Jean-Baptiste Du Halde (1674–1743) wrote a famous *Description of the Empire of China* (1735).

navigation of the other three parts of the world; as France, England and Holland, do nearly that of Europe.

Montesquieu, *The Spirit of Laws* (1748).

Read the free English text online (1793 edition):
https://books.google.co.uk/books?id=uxBVAAAAYAAJ
&pg=PA54

Read the free text in the original language (1748 edition):
http://classiques.uqac.ca/classiques/montesquieu/de_esprit_
des_lois/partie_4/esprit_des_lois_Livre_4.pdf

20. Religious Toleration

In his Project for Perpetual Peace in Europe, *the Abbé de Saint-Pierre addresses religious toleration and the dialogue between different communities, whether they are Catholic, Protestant, Muslim, or Orthodox.*

The union under discussion is not the rapprochement of different religions, but rather peace between nations of different religions. But then, is anything impossible? The Lutherans of Germany, for example, are they not at peace with the Catholics of Germany? Has a difference in religion prevented Spain from unifying with Holland? If we waged war only for religion, this objection would have meaning, but this project leaves to each his own religion, as it does all his other possessions. Hence, there is no need to reconcile all the nations of the world to this issue; I have only said, as I have said before, that if there are any human means that hope to bring diverse sects little by little closer to the truth, the establishment of perpetual peace is the most reliable of all those means. It is even the foundation of all conciliation. Through frequent exchange, opinions can be frequently compared, and it is only with the promise of frequent comparisons that we can hope that the most reasonable opinions will rise to the top in the end, and that reason will consequently serve to bring all men to the true religion. [...]

I have heard the objection that among Muslims, it is an article of faith to limit negotiation with Christians to truces, without ever making treaties, but those who speak thus are not well informed on an essential distinction. Although their faith prohibits making solid and resilient peace with Christian enemies who are their equals, or nearly equals, in strength, they are not forbidden from making solid and resilient peace with Christians who are irrevocably superior in strength, since it would put their faith in evident peril. Therefore, if the Sultan alone became the enemy of the European Society, would his Empire and his religion not be in clear danger? Moreover, since faith permits them to make truces lasting twenty years and then to renew them, do not these perpetually renewed truces come to the same end as a perpetual peace?

Charles-Irénée Castel de Saint-Pierre,
Project for Perpetual Peace in Europe (1713).

**Read the free text in the original language
(1713 edition, volume I):**
http://gallica.bnf.fr/ark:/12148/bpt6k86492n?rk=21459;2

**Read the free text in the original language
(1713 edition, volume II):**
http://gallica.bnf.fr/ark:/12148/bpt6k864930?rk=42918;4

21. The Riches of European Cuisine

Louis-Antoine Caraccioli, maintains in Paris, the Model of Foreign Nations, or French Europe *that French cuisine has contributed to a general enrichment of culinary habits in Europe. Thus, he offers a glimpse of the future importance of French gastronomy.*

On Dining

Nobody will contest that it is most certainly to the French that Europe owes both the inestimable honour of no longer drowning all good reason in wine, and the virtue of delicate dining. I know that the Italians never indulged in the excesses of drunkenness; but since they do not host grand dinners, and one of the principal virtues of Italian nobility is sobriety, we cannot attribute to them the glory of having banished drunkenness from banquets.

In years gone by, a foreigner who travelled to Germany and to Poland, and who found himself invited to dine with society's elite, would offend those present if he did not drink. He would be forced to follow the example of his companions, and to drink to the health of the living, and even of the dead; since by the end of the evening, few really knew what they were saying.

This strange custom has now been abolished, and were it not for the excellence and variety of wines that make German feasts superior to French banquets, it might be said that no more is drunk in Warsaw or in Prague than in Paris. Only the English are yet to relinquish this bad habit; which makes no small contribution to slowing down their progress in the sciences.

Whether through encounters with French ambassadors, or by visiting France themselves, foreigners have finally learned that temperance is the special virtue of the gentry, and if on occasion one might happen to sip the finest of wines, and reach a point of merriment, it is detestable to lose one's reason and senses. Nonetheless, we cannot deny that our meals have become rather tedious since we have been so concerned with intellectual conversation, and that it is only the delicious food that sustains them; but it is such excellent food…

How disagreeable it once was to dine among the Russians, but how free, and how pleasant is that experience now! Nowadays, they hold interesting conversations, laugh with ease, dine delicately, and this is yet another French miracle.

They have been supping in Milan, since Marshal de Villars introduced the custom of hosting dinners there; they feast in Turin as in a country that borders Grenoble and Lyons, and in Rome itself, following the good example set by French ambassadors, they are beginning to know what it is to eat delicious food, and at times, even to relish it.

'Please do me the honour of dining with me', a Neapolitan says amicably to a friendly traveller of his acquaintance. 'We will number fewer than the Muses but more than the Graces, just as many as are required for the conversation to be general and not too loud'.

'Ah!' replies the Foreigner, 'it is not a Neapolitan who invites me but a Frenchman: when one receives such a pleasant invitation, it is in Paris and not in Naples that one surely finds oneself'.

Louis-Antoine Caraccioli,
Paris, the Model of Foreign Nations, or French Europe (1777).

Read the free text in the original language (1777 edition):
http://gallica.bnf.fr/ark:/12148/bpt6k1156961

🔊 **Listen to the free audio book in the original language:**
http://gallica.bnf.fr/ark:/12148/bpt6k1156961/f3.vocal

22. Europe through Persian Eyes

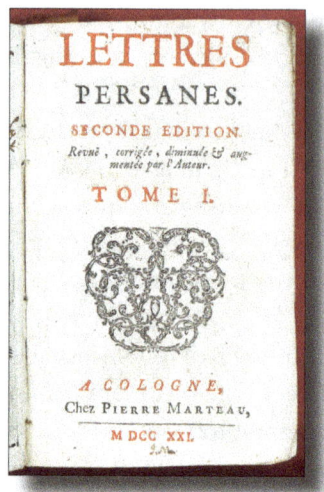

In his epistolary novel Persian Letters, *Montesquieu (1689–1755) shows France through the foreign gaze of two travellers from Isfahan, Rica and Usbek. In Europe, the Persians discover a variety of political regimes, which lead them to consider the government most in tune with reason. It is also a continent which has had diverse regimes on its soil, including republics. Rhedi speaks of a wind of liberty which comes from the north, and considers the way in which the love of freedom is rooted in the history of European republics.*

Rhedi to Rica, at Paris

One of the things which most exercised my curiosity after my arrival in *Europe*, was the history and origin of Republics. Thou knowest that generally the *Asiatics* have not so much as the least idea of this sort of government, and that their imagination never extended so far as to comprehend, there could possibly be any other sort than the despotic throughout the world.

The first governments were monarchical: it was only by chance, and length of time, that republics were formed.

Greece having been swallowed up by a deluge, new inhabitants came to people it: she had almost all her colonies from *Egypt*, and the nearest *Asiatic* countries: and those countries being governed by Kings, the people that came out of them were governed in the like manner. But the tyranny of those Princes growing too heavy, the people shook off the yoke, and from the broken remains of so many Kingdoms arose those Republics which made *Greece* so very flourishing, the only polite country amidst Barbarians.

The love of Liberty and aversion to Kings, preserved *Greece* a long time in a state of independence, and very far extended the Republican

Government. The cities of *Greece* found allies in *Asia Minor*: they sent thither colonies as free as themselves, which were so many ramparts against the attempts of the Kings of *Persia*. This was not all: *Greece* peopled *Italy*, *Italy Spain*, and perhaps *Gaul*. 'Tis notorious that the great *Hesperia*, so famous among the Ancients, was at the beginning *Greece*, which was looked upon by its neighbours as the seat of Felicity: the *Greeks* not finding at home that happy country, went and looked for it in *Italy*; those of *Italy*, in *Spain*; those of *Spain*, in *Bætica* or *Portugal*: so that all these regions went by this Name among the Ancients. These *Greek* colonies carried along with them a Spirit of Liberty, which they had assumed from that kindly climate. And accordingly we seldom or never, in those remote times, meet with monarchies in *Italy*, *Spain*, or either of the *Gauls*. We shall see by and by, that the people of the *North* and of *Germany* were no less free than the others; and if there are appearances of anything like Royalty among them, it is because their leaders of armies, or heads of Republics, were mistaken for Kings.

All this happened in *Europe*: as for *Asia* and *Africa* they were ever oppressed with despotism; excepting some towns of *Asia Minor* already taken notice of; and the republic of *Carthage* in *Africa*.

The World was divided between two powerful Republics, *Rome* and *Carthage*: nothing is so well known as the beginning of the *Roman* Republic, and nothing so little known as the origin of that of *Carthage*: we are utterly ignorant of the succession of the *African* Princes after *Dido*, nor do we know by what means they came to lose their Power. The prodigious increase of the *Roman* republic would have been a great blessing to mankind, had there not been that unreasonable difference between the citizens of *Rome* and the conquered Nations; had they given to the Governors of Provinces a more limited Authority; had they paid due regard to those divine laws made to restrain their tyranny; and had they not, in order to silence those *Laws*, employed the very treasures which their rapine and injustice had accumulated together.

Liberty seems to be calculated to the Genius of the Nations of *Europe*, and Slavery adapted to that of the *Asiatics*. In vain did the *Romans* offer that invaluable treasure to the *Cappadocians*; that worthless Nation refused it, and courted servitude with the same ardour as other Nations pursued Liberty.

Cæsar crushed the *Roman* Republic, and brought it under arbitrary Power.

Europe groaned a long time beneath the military and violent Government; and the *Roman* mildness was changed into a hard-hearted oppression.

Meanwhile infinite numbers of unknown Nations swarmed from out the *North*; spread themselves like torrents through all the *Roman* provinces; and finding it as easy a thing to make conquests, as to exercise their piracies, they dismembered those provinces and made Kingdoms of them. These people were free; and they so confined the authority of their Kings, that they were properly speaking no more than chieftains, or generals. Thus those Kingdoms, though founded in force, felt not the yoke of a conqueror. When the Nations of *Asia*, namely the *Turks* and the *Tartars*, made any conquests, they being accustomed to the will and pleasure of one single person, thought of nothing more than bringing him new subjects, and by the force of arms establish his violent authority: but the *Northern* Nations being free in their own country, when they had seized the *Roman* provinces, took care not to bestow on their chiefs too large a power. Nay, some of them, the *Vandals*, for instance, in *Africa*, the *Goths* in *Spain*, deposed their Kings whenever they were dissatisfied with them; and the others too abridged the authority of the Prince a thousand ways: a great number of Lords took share of it with him; a War was never entered upon without their Consent; the Plunder was divided between the General and the soldiers; no taxation in favour of the Prince; the laws were made in Assemblies of the whole Nation. Such was the fundamental principle of all those States that were formed out of the wrecks of the *Roman* Empire.

Venice, 20th of the Moon, Regeb, 1719.

Montesquieu, *Persian Letters* (1721).

Read the free English text online (1736 edition):
https://books.google.co.uk/books?id=rAE6AAAAcAAJ
&printsec=frontcover

Read the free text in the original language (1873 edition):
https://fr.wikisource.org/wiki/Lettres_persanes

23. Literature from the North to the South

Anne Louise Germaine de Staël-Holstein (1766–1817),[i] daughter of the banker Jacques Necker, who was a minister under Louis XVI, is the author of novels (Delphine, *1802;* Corinne, *1807) as well as of political and literary treatises. In her essay* Germany *(written in 1810 but first published in 1813), she introduced literature from across the Rhine to the French, and reflected on the national characters of both countries. The connections between literature and socio-historical contexts were already at the heart of her 1800 work* On Literature Considered in Relation to Social Institutions.

On Literature from the North

It seems to me that there are two completely distinct literatures: one from the Mediterranean and one from the North, one that has its source in Homer and one that originated with Ossian.[ii] The Greeks, Romans,

---

i   https://commons.wikimedia.org/wiki/File:Madame_de_Staël.jpg

ii   In 1760 a Scottish poet called James Macpherson (1736–1796) collected songs said to be by Ossian under the title *Fragments of Ancient Poetry, Collected in the Highlands of Scotland, and Translated from the Galic or Erse Language*. For Staël, these poems

Italians, Spanish and French from the century of Louis XIV belong to the literary genre that I shall call the literature of the South. The English, German and some Danish and Swedish writings must be classified as literature of the North. Before characterising the English and German writers, it seems to me necessary to consider more generally the principal differences between the two literary hemispheres. [...]

Climate is certainly one of the main reasons for the differences which exist between the images that are appealing in the North and those which people like to call to mind in the South. The daydreams of poets can give life to extraordinary things; but everything they create is inevitably shaped by impressions of ordinary experience. Avoiding the traces of these impressions would mean losing the greatest of advantages, that of depicting one's own experiences. Poets from the South constantly mingle images of coolness, dense woods and clear streams with all of life's emotions. They never simply go over the delights of the heart, without mingling them with an idea of benevolent shadows protecting them from the burning heat of the sun. Their natural surroundings, which are full of life, arouse in them impulses more than thoughts. It seems wrong to me that people have claimed passions were more violent in the South than in the North. You see more diverse interests in the South, but less intensity in individual ideas, when it is rather steadiness that produces miracles of passion and will. The peoples of the North are less concerned with pleasure than with pain, and their imagination is all the more fertile for it. [...]

The poetry of the North is more suited to the spirit of a free people than the poetry of the South. [...]

Philosophy, at the time of the literary renaissance, began in the northern countries, reason finding far fewer prejudices to fight against in their religious habits than it does in those of Mediterranean peoples.

In general, there is nothing so cold and artificial as religious dogmas exported to a country where they are seen merely as ingenious metaphors. The poetry of the North is rarely allegorical; none of the

---

seem to demonstrate the existence of a Nordic tradition comparable to the Homeric tradition. Current criticism sees these as compilations created by the supposed editor, without being able to determine precisely the extent to which they are based on an oral tradition or on possible documents.

effects rely on local superstitions to stir the imagination. A measured enthusiasm and a pure exaltation can suit all people equally well; it is the true poetic inspiration, whose sentiment exists in everyone's heart, but whose expression is the gift of genius.

Germaine de Staël,
On Literature Considered in Relation to Social Institutions (1800).

Read the free text in the original language (1800 edition):
http://gallica.bnf.fr/ark:/12148/bpt6k61078256/f2.image

 **Listen to the free audio book in the original language:**
http://gallica.bnf.fr/ark:/12148/bpt6k61078256/f2.vocal

24. Of National Characters

François-Ignace d'Espiard de La Borde (1707–1777) was the son of an eminent lawyer at the Parlement de Franche-Comté. He took holy orders. His only known work is his Essai sur le génie et le caractère des nations *(Essay on the Genius and Character of Nations), published in Brussels in 1743. A second edition came out in 1752 under the title* The Spirit of the Nations. *He considers the influence of physical factors, connected to geography, on national character and stresses that 'for a nation, climate is the fundamental cause of genius, to which must be added similar subordinate ones like the quality of the blood, the nature of the diet, the quality of the water and the vegetation'. He examines particular applications of his theory by taking into account women and love.*

All the several people inhabiting the earth, we divide into three parts. The first comprehends the thirty degrees northward from the Equator, which we shall assign to the southern and scorched regions; the thirty successive degrees till the sixtieth northwards, comprehend the middle and temperate countries; and the thirty from thence to the Pole shall be the degrees of the northern people, and the regions of excessive cold.

The same divisions are also to be observed from the Equator to the Antarctic Pole. [...]

In a more happy position, betwixt 40 and 50, are situated the hithermost parts of *Spain, France, Italy, Lower Germany* as far as the *Main, Hungary, Illyria,* both *Mysias,*[i] the country of the *Dacians,*[ii] *Moldavia, Turkey* in *Europe,* a great part of *Lesser Asia, Sogdania* bordering southwards on *Bactriana,* together with *Armenia* and the province of the *Parthians.* [...]

The *Americans* and *Europeans* are warlike people, who yet never shut up their women. The *Savages, Scythians, Goths,* etc. in all their Barbarity, so far from entertaining a thought of depriving them of their Liberty, admitted them in private concerns even to a kind of equality with Man.

---

i   The north-west of Asia Minor.
ii Romania.

Their happiness began in *Europe*, with the settlements of those people, that is, as soon as it could begin: The further North, the more female authority, and the less jealousy. The indifference of the *German* laws on this head would scarce be credited; yet these same *Visigoths*, afterwards penetrating into *Spain*, adapted the jealous laws of the Nation, and which in those climates are a matter of necessity, if the conduct of Women, who are indulged some freedom at *Cuzco, Lima, Goa*, and in the *Indies*, be not misrepresented by Travellers.

I leave the particulars of the *French* spirit of society, of manners and gallantry to the expatiations of the writers of these surprising adventures and ingenious novels: A philosophic view only agrees with our design, and this will exhibit a general idea of the mind and heart of different Nations in this article.

Beauty inspires either passion, sensual desires, gaiety, or admiration. The pensive and melancholy *Spaniard* tends more directly to the natural object of the passion, which is beauty, preferring it to wit and hilarity. The *Italian* already prevaricates: It is not the object of the passion, beauty, to which he directly tends, but to his scope, which is pleasure: He prefers a timorous beauty. The *Spaniard*'s passion is all nature: That of the *Italian* has in it something of imagination and wit.

The *Frenchman*, more superficial in his sentiments, is not so vehemently carried towards beauty; the woman of wit and gaiety takes more with him. The *German* is of another cast; in him beauty excites admiration and respect, which, however are not its essential effects; nor has all the beauty of the *German* women been able to disperse the phlegm of that Nation, or communicate to the style and arts that spirit and fire, in which *Italy* and *France* have so happily imitated Antiquity.

The mode of love, particular to each Nation, answers to its principle. The *Spaniard* is a madman; he threatens universal destruction, if he fails of his point; yet upon miscarrying, betakes himself to macerations, and all those amorous penances, which are so facetiously described in their romances. Fifty years ago there was, and may be still, at the court of *Spain*, a particular sect of these amorists, distinguished by the style of *Embevecidos* or *drunk with Love*; they are allowed their transports in public; their dress and behaviour, how extravagant soever [*sic*], are taken no notice of; love, by which they are entirely possessed, being an excuse for their madness.

The *Italian* makes his advances, under the images of a polite voluptuousness, and the most refined impudence: The terms and genius of his poetry tend to seducement [*sic*], and his passion breaks forth in music and concerts: No Nation comes up to him in poetical fecundity, he never gives over till he is a conqueror, or even revenged on his rival.

The *Frenchman* is volatile, sparkling and giddy. His gay passion makes use only of songs or railleries, ludicrous flights, balls, and collations; but he no sooner comes to be loved, than he immediately grows out of conceit with the object about which he took so much pains. If his mistress is insensible, he vents his spite in menaces and slander; but it is his happiness, that no storm is of any long continuance with him.

The wary, cold meditative *German* is not easily moved; but when once smitten, he pours in his presents; his gallantry understands nothing further; he is also timorous and confused, and scrupulously nice against the least breach of decency. If it be his happiness to be beloved, he presently cools; if he is slighted, he continues in love.

[…] These are the only four manners in which this passion operates; all the love systems of other Nations being reducible to these, either jointly or separately.

François-Ignace d'Espiard de La Borde, *The Spirit of Nations* (1752).

Read the free English text online (1753 edition):
https://books.google.co.uk/books?id=7YjTkxx12qAC&lpg=PA4
&dq=espiard de la borde earth three equator&hl=fr&pg=PA4

Read the free text in the original language (1753 edition):
https://books.google.co.uk/books?id=o2Q9AQAAMAAJ
&printsec=frontcover

25. Linguistic Diversity in Europe

In Paris, the Model of Foreign Nations, or French Europe, *Louis-Antoine Caraccioli notes the supremacy of the French language over the other European languages. He thus enters into a debate that engaged many other contemporary thinkers, including Rivarol.*

On Languages

The peoples of every nation express their character through their speech. Polish ease, German sincerity, Italian flexibility, Spanish vigour and French light-heartedness can be felt in their respective languages, and in the manner in which they are pronounced. Some people drag out their sentences, whilst others rush through them; where one man mumbles his words another pronounces each with a ringing clarity.

If I were to order each language according to its value, I would say that after Greek and Latin, both Italian, so evocative and sonorous, and French, so elegant and precise, deserve to be held in the greatest esteem. If the latter is now victorious, this is due to its concise and natural phrasing, which makes it the language of society; the Italian language, thanks to its harmonious features, seems far less suited to conversation than to music and poetry.

[...] When one seeks to converse, one must return to French; for, less wordy than any other language, and less difficult to pronounce, it neither requires verbosity nor any sustained vocal efforts to bring thoughts to life. In other words, it adorns them in such a manner as to render them most pleasant to hear, without vexing or inflating them.

If certain writers made the claim that it was imperfect, this was because they lacked the flair to do it justice, but it has defiantly avenged itself for these false accusations through the pleasure taken by Europeans when they speak it.

Let us all, then, write like Pascal, like Malebranche, Bossuet and Rousseau; and the public will soon be persuaded that the French language is truly rich, and that even if it does not provide an infinite number of different expressions, it nonetheless lends to thought a certain elegance and energy that mediocre authors do not believe possible.

Foreigners have felt this alluring charm, and have been led, in spite of themselves, to forget their own language in order to speak that of the French. It is astonishing to hear French conversation at the courts of Vienna, St Petersburg, or Warsaw, just as at that of Versailles. This is the very same language, spoken with the very same accent.

Frenchmen, reap the rewards of such an honour, and try more than ever to enrich this language, which has become almost universal.

The Parisian who travels across Europe may scarcely realise that he is away from Paris, since there is no city he visits in which people are unable to answer him.

This language has the advantage of having provided the English with almost all their scientific and artistic terminology. Those proud islanders, who do not want to owe anything to anyone, had no choice but to borrow a plethora of energetic words from the French; every season they swarm to France to learn the language of Corneille and Racine. For that is yet another advantage of the French language: to be able to rise to the most sublime heights of poetry, and to bring freshness to the most brilliant thoughts.

Louis-Antoine Caraccioli,
Paris, the Model of Foreign Nations, or French Europe (1777).

Read the free text in the original language (1777 edition):
http://gallica.bnf.fr/ark:/12148/bpt6k1156961

Listen to the free audio book in the original language:
http://gallica.bnf.fr/ark:/12148/bpt6k1156961/f3.vocal

26. The Role of Germany in European Culture

August Wilhelm Schlegel (1767–1845),[i] a German intellectual of the Romantic period who knew many other European thinkers like Germaine de Staël, looks at the role of German literature in European culture, in his critical treatise Abrisse von den europäischen Verhältnissen der deutschen Literatur *(Outline of the European Conditions of German Literature) (c.1828).*

Germany, despite being not only geographically but also intellectually at the heart of Europe, remains a *terra incognita* even for its immediate neighbours. And yet, this form of existence has its advantages: after all, princes travel *incognito*, finding it appealing to get to know people whilst remaining unrecognised by them? We are, I think I can say, the cosmopolitans of European culture: we rarely ask in what country some new truth has first come to light; no partisan considerations or narrowness of outlook prevents us from immediately acknowledging and using any discovery in the world of learning, wherever it was made. The exaggerated adulation of other nations has not made us vain, as has happened to the detriment of our neighbours to the west; this is the least of our grievances. On the other hand, we are equally unconcerned by their criticism: for we know in advance, that for the most part it arises out of unfamiliarity, or out of deep-seated prejudices and biased mental habits. […]

Modern Europe has come of age. We have taken possession of the rich intellectual patrimony left to us by Greece and Rome; we have been shaped by the Reformation and the long centuries of controversies it gave rise to, including some that at first sight appear to be unrelated to religious and ecclesiastical questions; shaped further by the extraordinary and historically unprecedented flowering of natural

---

i   https://www.flickr.com/photos/internetarchivebookimages/14777435381

history and natural science; and finally by the discoveries made of
continents and oceans, begun by Vasco da Gama and Columbus, and
now nearly complete, which have led to familiarity and indeed active
commerce with the entirety of the human inhabitants of our planet.

August Wilhelm Schlegel,
Outline of the European Conditions of German Literature (*c*.1828).

Louis-Léopold Boilly, *The Coach's Arrival in the Cour des Messageries* (1803).[ii]

---

ii   https://commons.wikimedia.org/wiki/File:Louis-Léopold_Boilly_002.jpg

27. The Rape of Europa

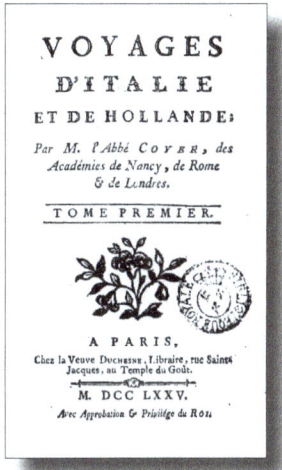

Until 1736, Gabriel Coyer (1707–1782), was a Jesuit. He then became a tutor and private secretary as well as a man of letters in his own right. His ideas are often original and audacious. He was on the side of the 'philosophes' in many great Enlightenment debates, to the extent that Voltaire said of him: 'He is one of our brothers'. He visited Italy in 1763–1764 and Holland in 1769.[i]

Venice, June 12th 1764

You have seen the rape of Europa everywhere. Paolo Veronese also painted it; but what art in his grouping of the figures, what shades of colours, what superiority! Never was the effect so striking, so beautiful. The Bull is licking the feet of the ravished Beauty. What do you think of this pleasing idea? The Palazzo of San Marco owns this treasure.

Gabriel Coyer, *Voyage Through Italy and Holland* (1775).

Read the free text in the original language (1775 edition):
http://gallica.bnf.fr/ark:/12148/bpt6k103467z

---

i   http://gallica.bnf.fr/ark:/12148/bpt6k103467z

28. An Economic Union

In the Project for Perpetual Peace in Europe, *Charles-Irénée Castel de Saint-Pierre defies any critics of the European project by emphasizing the impact of an economic union on the prosperity of participating nations.*

Claude-Joseph Vernet, *Coastal Scene*.[i]

People have said that if the unifying treaty increases trade for France, Spain, Denmark, Portugal, and others, the improvement could only happen to the detriment of England and especially of Holland, who are currently the two greatest hubs of business of the Earth. Nevertheless, it is simple enough to respond to this particular objection, and demonstrate that improvement for some need not harm the commerce of others; the truth is that business will expand for all the nations, though it will

---

i   https://commons.wikimedia.org/wiki/File:Vue_côtière.jpg

expand proportionally for all. The twelfth nation belonging to the European economic community will increase its trade; but since all the others will also increase trade proportionally, it will remain only the twelfth trading party. That which alone composed a third of this trade, likewise augmented, will continue to be a third of the total. Thus, the nations best equipped for doing trade will retain the greatest portion of the business.

Charles-Irénée Castel de Saint-Pierre,
Project for Perpetual Peace in Europe (1713).

Read the free text in the original language (1713 edition, volume I):
http://gallica.bnf.fr/ark:/12148/bpt6k86492n?rk=21459;2

Read the free text in the original language (1713 edition, volume II):
http://gallica.bnf.fr/ark:/12148/bpt6k864930?rk=42918;4

29. A Common European Market

Standing in stark contrast to the autarkic dream expressed by Johann Gottlieb Fichte in Der geschlossene Handelsstaat *(1800), Charles de Villers (1765–1815)[i] shows the need for a European common market which would bring together the major trading towns of northern and southern Europe. These towns, ports on rivers or seas, serve two commercial functions: one, direct, for the benefit of the local economic basin; the other, indirect, for the benefit of the whole continent. The term* Entrepôt *(warehouse), which is related to this second function, describes the commercial link between the northern and southern zones. The most favourable political model for trade is drawn from the three Hanseatic cities of Bremen, Hamburg and Lubeck, and should be applied to other cities, especially Italian cities such as Venice or Genoa. Finally, commercial activity, because it is noble in its purpose, requires vast knowledge. Villers dreams of an enlightened trader.*

The real and artificial needs of its inhabitants, their high degree of activities and civilisation, mean that they rely heavily on the reciprocal exchanges of the production of their soil and industry. One part of the continent abounds in wines, oils, exquisite fruits, silks, or wool, both raw and manufactured, and finally in aromatic and luxury goods—another one is abundant in grains, flax, and hemp (used to make tackle, canvas, rigging, etc.), in wood, in iron, in brass, in tar, tallow, and much more. In short, the climate, the soil, and the type of local industry make each region superabundant in one or several kinds of commodities, and completely lacking in a few others. Hence this exchange of what one has too much of, in order to obtain what one lacks. One who has an overabundance of wine can use it to procure grain; one with an overabundance of grain can procure wine in return. One who has too much metal uses it to buy grain and wine, etc. And it is in vain that

---

i   https://commons.wikimedia.org/wiki/File:Charles_de_Villers.jpg

each area, rebellious against nature, would seek to isolate itself from the others, and force its own soil to provide it with the various productions it needs. [...]

This is what constitutes the *second* commercial function, that of the *Entrepôt*; a function of the highest importance, which binds nations that are distant to one another, seemingly forbidden by nature to engage in direct commerce, at least to a certain degree of activity. The trade of any port which dominates a river consists in the direct sale of the own commodities of its fluvial plains, and in the purchase of whatever it consumes in foreign commodities. But the *Entrepôt* does not participate by itself, as regards production, in the object of its activity. On the other hand, it is merchandise from foreign and distant countries that it accumulates in its stores, receiving some to exchange for the others, and offering only a guarantee in legal currency, in good faith and skill. The business of the *Entrepôt* is therefore intended to be *indirect*, and not limited to imports and exports from a single commercial province. The first function of commerce, ever referring only to a limited district, is local, and almost always restricted to a single nation; the latter encompasses masses of whole states; it serves the interests of all, and establishes systems of power, which are to be sacred to all nations participating in their beneficent influence. [...]

That which is necessary to all, which belongs to all, must belong to no one in particular. The great trading *Entrepôts* are the common property of all Europe; and it must henceforth be an inviolable article of international law in this part of the world, that in all the wars to come the absolute neutrality of these places must be respected, and that neither their lands, nor their ports, nor their premises should be touched, that no armed troops should be allowed to pass through their walls, and that no one should be permitted to draw any contributions from them. These arrangements must not be dictated by any sense of favour towards the Hanseatic towns; but by the general interest of all, and by a spirit of noble civilisation, which takes upon itself the duty of guaranteeing that attainment of all that has been put into place to make it flourish. [...]

These first lines of a general organisation of European trade show how the particular functions of the individual members of this great ensemble are precise and determined by the state of affairs. In order for each one to make the best possible use of their position and state of affairs, they must know both as well as possible, and not blindly adhere to routine. The merchant must be educated, and well educated! The perfect knowledge of the land, its productions, its inhabitants, its various languages, law, history, politics, finance, travel, and so many others are absolutely indispensable. For the trade to flourish and grow, it must be guided by enlightened perspectives and ideals. Unfortunately many traders are lacking in this regard. I have seen some who even displayed contempt for education. It is very desirable that a change should take place in this matter. The establishment of an *Academy of Trade* would be of great benefit to all Europe. Hamburg would be the ideal location. This academy could be placed in the small town of Bergedorf, near the banks of the Elbe, which is shared by Hamburg and Lubeck. Such an institution would be worthy of a city that has produced such men as Büsch, Reimarus, Ebeling, etc.

Charles de Villers, *Constitutions of the Three Free-Hanseatic Towns, Lubeck, Bremen and Hambourg, with a Memorandum on the Rank these Towns Should Occupy in Europe's Commercial Organisation* (1814).

Read the free text in the original language (1814 edition):
https://books.google.co.uk/books?id=deBYAAAAcAAJ
&printsec=frontcover

30. The Empire of Reason

The political thought of Stanislaus Leszczynski (1677–1766),[i] King of Poland and later Duke of Lorraine, combines pragmatism and idealism. In order to live in peace with its neighbours, a state must be able to make itself feared, but its empire will only be made durable through the wisdom of its laws and the virtue of its sovereign. In his Conversation Between a European and an Islander from the Kingdom of Dumocala, *Stanislaus stages a dialogue between a voyager, shipwrecked off an uncharted southern island, and a venerable old man, 'a kind of Brahmin', whom he encounters on his third day there.*

'You are mistaken', resumed the Brahmin. 'True, our island may be isolated, yet it is vast. Only the main part belongs to us, and naturally our neighbours must envy our power, especially since not one of them can rival it. While hardly formidable on their own, they could, were they to unite, become so; but our political system shields us from their affronts. Our honest dealings have won us their trust, and they have had such abundant proof of our even-handedness that they believe us to be at least as capable of safeguarding their peace as they are.

Amongst themselves they are less at ease, owing to their mutual suspicion, such that they are almost constantly attacking one another; and since they are so evenly matched in strength, outright victory is never achieved, making their wars relentless and thus all the more cruel.

It is only through the ascendancy we have over them, conferred on us by the esteem in which they hold our wisdom, that we can put an end to their plight. They recognise our Sovereign as the arbiter of their disputes; and, while powerful enough, it should be said, to impose peace upon them, he derives greater glory from bestowing this peace

---

i   https://commons.wikimedia.org/wiki/File:Atelier_de_Van_Loo-Portrait_de_Stanislas_Leszczynski-Musée_barrois.jpg

than he would by exploiting their weariness so as to extend, to their detriment, the boundaries of his own empire.

Herein lies a kind of Universal Monarchy, one whose foundations are all the stronger as the very nations whom it subjugates are the more willing to submit to it than the peoples governed by these nations are to obey their laws.

Whence it follows that in order to preserve this monarchy such as they desire it, our troops are always ready to march wherever the need arises. But contrary to the customs of your own lands, these troops, whose sole purpose in waging war is to end it, do not raise against us those nations, who, while deriving benefit from our supremacy, are prepared, should we try abuse it, to join forces so as to put it asunder, yet who rather seek to maintain this supremacy, since truly our only interest is to render it beneficial to them.

So compare now your polity with our own', the Brahmin went on, 'and see which is the worthier, the surer, indeed the more advantageous: either one which cannot but arouse suspicion, as it only ever succeeds through its efforts to conceal itself, or one which, displaying itself in the open, serves to other nations as an example of harmony and good will, rather than an emblem of mistrust and fear'.

Stanislaus Leszczynski, *Conversation Between a European and an Islander from the Kingdom of Dumocala* (1752).

Read the free text in the original language (1752 edition):
http://gallica.bnf.fr/ark:/12148/bpt6k84469n

31. The Circulation of Riches

Tomás de Iriarte (1750–1791)[i] was a Spanish aristocrat brought up in a family which displayed great interest in French culture. He was to build on this tradition as he became a celebrated translator, in particular of French plays. His fables crossed the Pyrenees in the other direction since they greatly influenced Jean-Pierre Claris de Florian, a late-eighteenth-century French fabulist. This text shows that no-one is a prophet in his or her own land, but also that what comes from elsewhere should always be made welcome.

Fable XLI – Tea and Sage

Tea met Sage on the road from Imperial China. She said to him: 'Where are you headed, kind sir?' 'I'm going to Europe, kind lady, where I know they will spend a pretty penny to have me'.

---

i   https://commons.wikimedia.org/wiki/File:Tomas_de_Iriarte_Joaquin_Inza.jpg

Sage replied: 'I am going to China, where, for my flavour and medicine, they shall receive me with the greatest esteem. In Europe, they treat me like some weed, and I have never been able to make my fortune'.

'Fare thee well. Your journey will not be in vain, for there is no nation that does not shower praise and wealth upon any foreign thing'.

Tomás de Iriarte, *Literary Fables* (1782).

Read the free text in the original language:
http://albalearning.com/audiolibros/iriarte/41te.html

🔊 **Listen to the free audio book in the original language:**
http://albalearning.com/SONIDO/iriarte/albalearning-41te_iriarte.mp3

32. European Sociability

Louis-Antoine Caraccioli describes in his treatise Paris, the Model of Foreign Nations, or French Europe, *how the model of French sociability through conversation has contributed to civilising all of Europe.*

On the Mind of Society

That affable and easy disposition, which gains trust and is well liked in all countries, is not given to all men. I know only of the Italians, the French and perhaps the Swedish who have it in themselves to approach those they meet, and who speak to them willingly.

Europeans, almost all of them reserved, have only become communicative since they adopted French manners. In years gone by, an incredible effort was required to squeeze just one word out of an Englishman. Always convinced that his interlocutor was trying to catch him out, he would search for the shortest monosyllable to wrench himself out of such an awkward situation, and he repaid everyone who tried to converse with him in this way.

But it was an entirely different case when one went to his country. He no longer recognised people who had been extremely polite towards him. What a century! Everything has changed, the Dutch speak, and the English welcome foreigners.

By dint of hearing the French chatter, others copy them without realising. Moreover, because they are naturally inquisitive and curious, the French frequently ask so many questions that, willingly or not, their interlocutors are forced to respond. Through this process, tongues have been loosened, and now the art of conversation is known everywhere in Europe.

These are no longer the days of men spending an entire day smoking together, without uttering a single word. Dutch smoking parlours have become almost as noisy as if they were full of Frenchmen, and German inns, where one would formerly receive only a strained response, now often have hosts who will mutter a few sentences, and even manage some compliments.

I admit that the Frenchman has a tendency to intervene in discussions; that often, without knowing those standing before him, he speaks to them; even asks them questions, and that he seeks to become the friend of all humankind. But is that not better than being a morose character, with the air of a statue escaped from a Mausoleum; or a man who always believes himself to be in enemy territory, and who fears compromising himself, even when only talking about the rain? I prefer a giddy, babbling creature to a cynic who does not say a word; I'd dine with my parrot just as gladly as I'd dine with a strange fellow who only unclenches his teeth to put food in his mouth.

What is more pleasant for a man who travels, than meeting people who discuss various events with him, who tell him the news of the day, who tell him the stories from the day before, and who declare themselves to be his friends, his brothers, from the moment they chance upon each other? [...]

We like to fancy the whole world as one and the same family, as fulfilling the same objectives and reaching the same goal, via their various occupations and their different tastes. In that sense we would say that there is only one mind, only one soul, and only one being.

Not fifty years ago a Frenchman introducing himself in some assembly, whether in Genoa or in London, would come across as a true lunatic. His free demeanour, his natural conversation would revolt people who knew only how to be serious. But now that we know the value of society, we no longer pass such baseless judgements. What was then taken as folly now passes as gaiety.

The art of conversation has always been France's favourite science: the French would sooner not exist, than not speak; and I do not feel that they are wrong, since word and thought are essentially what distinguish men from animals.

The laws of conversation being to not dwell on any one subject, but to pass lightly from one topic to another, without effort and without affectation; to know how to speak of frivolous and serious matters; to remember that every exchange is a distraction, and not a bout of fencing; a game and not a study, the French are more proficient than any other nation at this type of exercise.

[...] There is nothing more delightful than knowing how to hold polite, gentle, light-hearted conversation, and it is a pleasure that today we find all over Europe. In Germany, and most of all in Italy, we mingle at gatherings where the soul is at ease, where the mind takes flight, where Minerva jests, where Venus moralises, where the Graces and the Muses fence beautifully; the Frenchman is happy there, for he finds Paris again, he finds himself again.

The Englishman, too, is acquiring this amiability, which is so interesting and so natural; today he does not even wish to be suspected of being distant and aloof. One might say that he is ashamed of ever having been so. The odds are that after the metamorphoses that we are seeing, he will finally be persuaded that amusement is not to be found in having feasts from the morning until the evening, or in giving in to immoderate raptures.

Following the example set by France, Europeans no longer converse as before, only to argue and to make a weapon out of erudition. Controversy is left to the schoolroom, and pedants are excluded from good company, where there are no longer theses to defend.

Louis-Antoine Caraccioli,
Paris, the Model of Foreign Nations, or French Europe (1777).

Read the free text in the original language (1777 edition):
http://gallica.bnf.fr/ark:/12148/bpt6k1156961

Listen to the free audio book in the original language:
http://gallica.bnf.fr/ark:/12148/bpt6k1156961/f3.vocal

33. The Safety of Europe's Borders

In the Project for Perpetual Peace in Europe, *Charles-Irénée Castel de Saint-Pierre envisions protections for the borders of Europe based on the mutual support of the associated members of the Union. Each nation would maintain its own troops, but they would be made available to allies.*

For the security of the Union, the Tsar would fortify all the borders close to the Princes who would not belong to the Union, and would maintain considerable garrisons composed of troops from the unified sovereigns.

If any neighbour should show unusual mobilisation, the Union would arm itself proportionally on that border, with one-third more troops than the neighbour. And lest the troops of the neighbouring sovereigns become more accustomed to war than the Union's troops, should these Princes make war, the Union will offer mediation, arbitration, and security for the current contentions, and will side with the party which accepts.

All will agree that in order to keep abreast of any new mobilisations, there will be ambassadors and residents dwelling within one another's countries.

The Emperor of the Turks will keep the same manner of conduct at the borders he shares with the Princes, who have not entered into the Union.

Charles-Irénée Castel de Saint-Pierre,
Project for Perpetual Peace in Europe (1713).

**Read the free text in the original language
(1713 edition, volume I):**
http://gallica.bnf.fr/ark:/12148/bpt6k86492n?rk=21459;2

**Read the free text in the original language
(1713 edition, volume II):**
http://gallica.bnf.fr/ark:/12148/bpt6k864930?rk=42918;4

34. Colonial Europe

Marie Leprince de Beaumont (1711–1780?)[i] was a novelist, a journalist and a pedagogue. She wrote educational dialogues like the Magasin des enfants *or* Young Misses' Magazine *(1756) and the* Magasin des adolescents *or* Young Ladies' Magazine *(1760) which suggested wide-ranging teaching models for girls, extending to the study of religion, of biology, of physics, of history, of law, of philosophy and so on. In this geography lesson about America, the governess, Mrs Affable, addressing herself to young pupils, is implicitly denouncing European colonialism and defending cultural relativity.*

Miss Sophie

Mrs Affable, I have heard there are tribes which kill their fathers once they are old, and then eat them. Is that true?

Mrs Affable

The Iroquois people who live in North America used to do so, but now they no longer do. Children, do not think they did this out of unkindness. Quite the opposite: When the Europeans came to their land and they found out that we let old people continue living and then bury them, they judged us to be very cruel. How barbarous, they said, to let those who gave us life suffer, and then to throw them into a hole in the ground where they are eaten by worms. We have much more love for our parents, they added: we spare them the discomforts of extreme old age and we give them our stomach as their tomb.

Marie Leprince de Beaumont, *The Young Ladies' Magazine, or Dialogues Between a Discreet Governess and Several Young Ladies of the First Rank Under Her Education*[ii] (1760).

---

i   https://commons.wikimedia.org/wiki/File:Jeanne-Marie_Leprince_de_Beaumont.jpg
ii   http://gallica.bnf.fr/ark:/12148/bpt6k5773041g

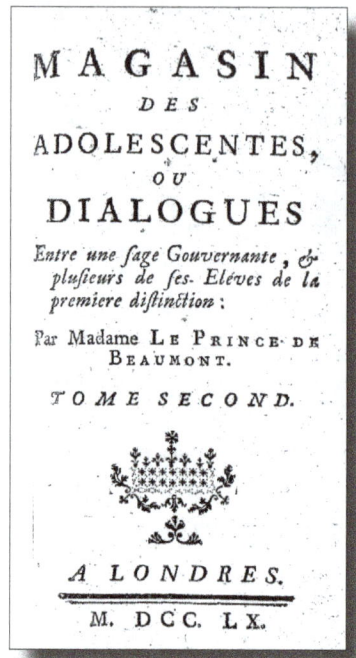

35. Another Vision of Education?

The Duke of Nivernais (1716–1798),[i] was a sometime poet and wrote numerous fables. One of them imagines an exchange between a 'savage' and a westerner. He evokes a form of physical harm, seen through European eyes, but also inner trauma pointed out in the primitive man's comments as he displays a form of wisdom his interlocutor does not possess.

Ill-Treated Heads

A savage kneaded,
Slimmed down, shrunk
An infant's head, to give it the shape
His tribe prized.[ii]
A European passing by
Found this barbarous indeed;
And chiding the American,
Criticised him for insulting
Nature's wise laws
By spoiling the human face.
The external shape may be damaged;
That I agree, said the Huron.
But we allow full scope to reason,
We do not hamper thought.
On your continent, it is said,
Judgment is narrowed

---

i   https://commons.wikimedia.org/wiki/File:Ardell_(d'après_Ramsay)_-_Louis_
      Jules_Barbon_Mazarini_Mancini.jpg
ii   See the accounts of all the travellers to America [author's note].

As the skull is narrowed here.
So which I prithee say to me,
Should truly be condemned?

Louis-Jules Barbon Mancini-Mazarini-Nivernois,
Duke of Nivernais, *Fables* (1796).

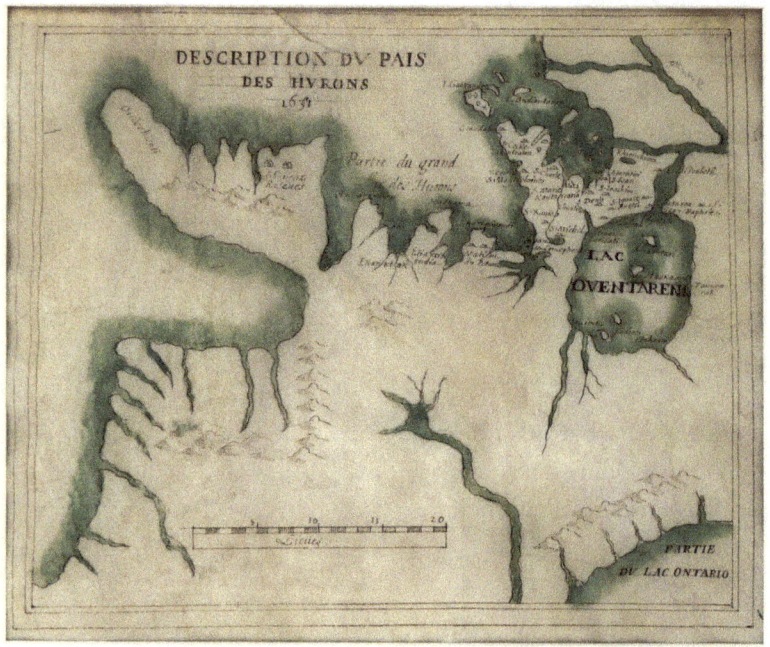

Anon. (possibly Jean de Brébeuf), *Map of Huron Country* (1631–1651).[iii]

Read the free text in the original language (1796 edition):
https://archive.org/details/fablesdemancinin02nive

---

iii   https://commons.wikimedia.org/wiki/File:Map_of_Huron_Country,_1631–51_
      WDL9557.png

36. The Importance of Trade

Like the Abbé de Saint Pierre or Montesquieu, Louis-Antoine Caraccioli, in his book on Paris as 'the model of foreign nations', underlines the importance of trade to further understanding between nations. In the second part of the eighteenth century, increased exchanges led to a transcultural Europe under France's aegis.

On Commerce

As commerce links Nations, it is hardly surprising it has done much to make Europe French. The Dutch and the English have without a doubt given it more consistency and scope than any other people, but the French have made it more active—it is well known that they have always liked movement.

I can see them on all the seas, sometimes quarrelling with destinies, sometimes with the elements, in order to amass goods, not so much, it must be said, to gain wealth as to shine. Their insinuating speech, their elegant air serve as their passport to reach the heart of those they wish to win over. It takes less time for them to subjugate a foreigner than for an Englishman to speak. Women, in particular, cannot deny them friendship, and that is why they so often marry in foreign lands and are never uncomfortable there.

Their manners are felt to be easy and marine trade, which generally renders customs harsh, makes them neither rude nor uncouth: perhaps because of the temperature of the air, perhaps because of the Nation's character, one who was born and brought up in France is rarely brutal. You encounter petulant men there, but never fierce ones.

It was thus through trade that the French tamed Europe. Good at insinuating themselves, they make proselytes even when apparently only dealing with trading questions.

[…] I am only referring here to the second class of tradesmen, as there are traders in all the major cities, like Nantes, Rouen, Lyons, Marseille, Bordeaux and of course Paris, who have sharp analyses, extensive knowledge, a love of the Muses—and indeed would be secretaries to them if their correspondence was as remunerative as that of Plutus.

Nothing sends man out into all the regions of the world like commerce. In his study, the tradesman converses with all the peoples in the world, ordering his letters to go out to Asia or else to America, to express his wishes; like the Sibyl's leaves of which Virgil speaks, I imagine them spreading all over and following the impetuous winds and waters.

It is through the tradesman that gold circulates, that pleasure and utility can march hand in hand, and that France displayed its fashion, its courtesies and its industry in all countries.

It is striking how much manufacturers have contributed to the fortunate change of which this book speaks. They attracted foreigners' attention thanks to the beauty of their work. There is not a court in Europe in which French fabrics are not fashionable. They flatter the vanity of the powerful, the frivolity of women; they shine on feast days. A dress which has not been made in Lyons, a diamond which has not been set in Paris, a fan which was not born there, are insipid objects for the foreigner. He only thrives when he spies some sample of French genius.

So, ingenious people of Lyons and elegant Parisians, work on! All you do will be praised as a masterpiece, such is the trust in your talent. It must be said that the smallest bagatelle which your hands produce bears the hallmark of delicacy and taste. That is why your name flies beyond the Alps and the Pyrenees and L'Empereur, and Germain, and du Lac,[i] etc. etc. are known even in the depths of Russia.

Louis-Antoine Caraccioli,
Paris, the Model of Foreign Nations, or French Europe (1777).

Read the free text in the original language (1777 edition):
http://gallica.bnf.fr/ark:/12148/bpt6k1156961

🔊 **Listen to the free audio book in the original language:**
http://gallica.bnf.fr/ark:/12148/bpt6k1156961/f3.vocal

---

i   The Germains were a dynasty of goldsmiths. Lempereur and the Dulacs—as their names are more usually spelled—sold luxury goods in Paris.

37. The Diversity and Unity of Europe

Johann Gottfried Herder (1744–1803),[i] was a German poet, philosopher and translator. He developed his philosophy of history in a treatise called Ideen zur Philosophie der Geschichte der Menschheit (Ideas on the Philosophy of the History of Humanity, *1784–1791). Here he shows that Europe's diversity is often a strength. The thinker is also conscious of eurocentrism and defends the idea of cultural relativity.*

Why does Europe distinguish itself in the differences between its nations, in the variety of its customs and art, and most of all in the influences that it has exerted over every other part of the world? I am well aware that many factors have come together, and that we will not be able to pick them all apart here; in physical terms, however, it is undeniable that its landscape, segmented and multi-form, has sparked and catalysed this process. When the peoples of Asia travelled here at different times and along different paths: what bays and coves, how many rivers, each flowing in a different way, what a variety of small mountain ranges they found here! They could be together and apart, interact with one another and leave each other in peace once more; this multifaceted small continent thus became, in microcosm, the market and gathering place of all the earth's peoples. The Mediterranean Sea, the only one of its kind, how much it has come to define Europe as a whole! So that one can almost say that this sea alone has formed the bridge of all ancient and medieval civilisations, and fostered their advancement. The Baltic Sea is by far its inferior because it lies further north, between harsh nations and barren lands, a side street of the global market as it were; but at the same time the eye with which the whole of northern Europe sees. Without it, most of its surrounding countries would be barbaric, cold, and uninhabitable. The same goes for the demarcation between Spain and France, for the Channel that separates the latter from England, for the shape of England, Italy, and of ancient Greece. If one were to alter

---

i   https://commons.wikimedia.org/wiki/File:Johann_Gottfried_Herder_2.jpg

the borders of these countries, remove a strait here, close off another there, for centuries the formation and destruction of the world, the fate of whole peoples and continents, would take a different course. [...]

I do not wish to stray any further into Europe. It is so rich and mixed in forms: in so many different ways has it varied nature through its art and culture that I will not venture to generalize about its subtly intermingled nations.

Johann Gottfried Herder,
Ideas on the Philosophy of the History of Humanity (1784–1791).

Read the free text in the original language (1786 edition):
https://books.google.co.uk/books?id=GegOAAAAQAAJ
&printsec=frontcover

38. A Critique of European Moress

In her epistolary novel, Letters from a Peruvian Woman, *which was published in 1747 and revised in 1752, Françoise de Graffigny (1695–1758)[i] basing her work on the model of Montesquieu's* Persian Letters, *formulates a criticism of western civilisation, and in particular of French mores. The letters of her heroine Zilia, who is doubly foreign in eighteenth-century French society, both as a woman and as a Peruvian, denounce the inequality of conditions in pre-revolutionary Europe.*

Letter 20 [extract]

Intent only about the afflictions of my heart, I have hitherto, my dear Aza, said nothing to thee respecting those of my understanding: yet these are not the less cruel because I have omitted them. I experience a distress of a nature unknown among us, and which nothing but the equivocal genius of this nation [France] could invent.

The government of this empire, quite opposite to that of thine, must necessarily be defective. With us, the Capa Inca[ii] is obliged to provide for the subsistence of his people: here, the sovereigns subsist only on the labours of their subjects: hence it is that most of the crimes and misfortunes of these people proceed from unsatisfied necessities.

The misfortunes of the nobles, in general, arise from the difficulties they are under to reconcile their apparent magnificence with their real misery.

The common people support their condition by what is called Commerce, or industry; the least evil arising from which is insincerity.

Part of the people, in order to live, are obliged to depend on the humanity of others; and this is so slender, that scarce have those wretches sufficient to preserve their existence.

Françoise de Graffigny, *Letters of a Peruvian Princess* (1747–1752).

---

i   https://commons.wikimedia.org/wiki/File:Françoise_d'Happencourt_de_Graffigny.png

ii The Inca sovereign.

Frontispiece of the 1752 edition of the *Letters of a Peruvian Princess,* drawn by
Eisen and engraved by Lafosse.[iii]

Read the free English text online (1787 edition):
https://books.google.co.uk/books?id=Gd1IAQAAMAA
J&dq=aza capa inca men peru&hl=fr&pg=PA29

Read the free text in the original language (1777 edition):
http://gallica.bnf.fr/ark:/12148/bpt6k62721455

 Listen to the free audio book in the original language:
http://gallica.bnf.fr/ark:/12148/bpt6k62721455/f4.vocal

---

iii   https://commons.wikimedia.org/wiki/File:Lettre_d'une_peruvienne_-_Skoklosters
      slott-_86192.tif

39. European Civilisation

David Hume (1711–1776),[i] a Scottish philosopher and historian, was famous in his own lifetime. His works were translated in different European languages. His Political Discourses *(1752) include a description of certain characteristics of European civilisation, including sociability, which he considers to be the sign of an advanced civilisation.*

Of Luxury

The more these refined arts advance, the more sociable do men become; nor is it possible, that, when enriched with science, and possessed of a fund of conversation, they should be contented to remain in solitude, or live with their fellow citizens in that distant manner, which is peculiar to ignorant and barbarous nations. They flock into cities; love to receive and communicate knowledge; to show their wit or their breeding; their taste in conversation or living, in cloths or furniture. […] Particular clubs and societies are everywhere formed: Both sexes meet in an easy and sociable manner, and men's tempers, as well as behaviour, refine apace. So that beside the improvements they receive from knowledge and the liberal arts, 'tis impossible but they must feel an increase of humanity, from the very habit of conversing together, and contributing to each other's pleasure and entertainment. Thus *industry, knowledge* and *humanity* are linked together by an indissoluble chain, and are found, from experience as well as reason, to be peculiar to the more polished and luxurious ages. […]

The bounds of all the *European* kingdoms are, at present, pretty near the same they were two hundred years ago: But what a difference is

---

i   https://commons.wikimedia.org/wiki/File:David_Hume.jpg

there in the power and grandeur of those kingdoms? Which can be ascribed to nothing but the increase of art and industry.

David Hume, *Political Discourses* (1752).

Read the free text online (1752 edition):
https://books.google.co.uk/books?id=fR9YAAAAcAAJ
&pg=PA27

40. The Progress of Justice in Europe

Lodovico Antonio Muratori (1672–1750) was an Italian historiographer and philosopher whose 1749 Treatise on Public Happiness[i] *was read throughout Europe. He proposed moderate political reforms and attempted to conciliate Enlightenment and catholicism. Here he salutes the advanced level of development in matters of justice in Europe.*

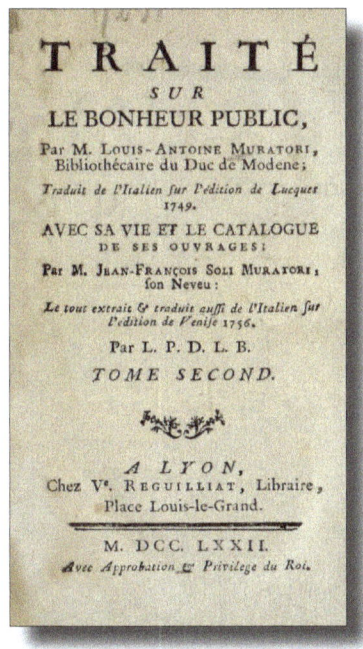

Poor Truth! We praise it abroad, and abhor it at home. Yet the endeavour of the Political Physician is indeed a dangerous one, and I would venture to say that the World prefers to go on limping, rather than to suffer those who, in civic matters, would teach it to walk straight. It should be added that, in some countries, any innovation whatsoever is unwelcome, if not abhorred or forbidden; almost as though, if there are bad innovations, there cannot be any really good ones, or even excellent ones to universal benefit. The customary pattern of living, thinking and ruling, as we

---

i   https://archive.org/details/traitsurlebonh02mura

found it at birth, is what we think best to pass on to our descendants in turn. Thus some people dislike the idea of Public Evils being pointed out, much as removing them is important; and similarly others dislike that the Best should be taught, much as introducing it would be beneficial. I have no more to say here, other than, the World having recently become much less rusty in most of Europe, and God having granted us good and well-intentioned Principles, it is to be wished that He now inspire in the World a sincere desire to know well that which is permissible and that which is not; and to know what harms the People so as to remedy it, and what can bring benefit, so as to embrace it. […]

On Jurisprudence

And as to making those indicted for grievous crimes to swear they are telling the truth, this has finally led many Christian Princes to order that this custom be ended, as if repugnant to the right of Nature. Finally, I will say that it is so important to the Happiness of a People to have good Justice administered, that glory will come to that Prince who will be constantly alert to this, or keep others alert; and who will also cast his watchful eye on to Advocates, Attorneys, and Notaries, so that such professions be entrusted solely to persons of upright conscience and sufficient knowledge, and that those who betray public trust may be punished.

Lodovico Antonio Muratori, *Treatise on Public Happiness* (1749).

Read the free text in the original language (1749 edition):
https://archive.org/details/bub_gb_3SRnd5k3HHsC

41. Bringing Europeans Together

Louis-Antoine Caraccioli, in the conclusion of his work Paris, The Model of Foreign Nations, or French Europe *identifies a fruitful coming together of European peoples in the eighteenth century. He attributes this to more frequent commerce between nations. Thus, the ideas of the Enlightenment thinkers, such as tolerance, circulated more widely. He observes with a certain satisfaction the supremacy of French taste which seems to be establishing itself throughout Europe.*

Oh! I breathe again. For Europe is now the most agreeable residence in the universe. I no longer see there the thickets, the marshes, the cliffs which injured the view, which despaired the traveller. The richest countryside, the most joyous lawns, the most beautiful view, the most beautiful roads. That is what I perceive, and it is France which has contributed more than any other country to this happy metamorphosis.

And what have we done to achieve such success? Both great and small things, as I have observed. The remedies most meagre in appearance are often the greatest help.

There is nothing more advantageous than to have crossed, by means of public ways and posts, the immense breach which separated Europeans from one another. It seems that there is no longer distance between us. Paris touches Petersburg, Rome Constantinople, and we are but one and the same family living in different regions. I call up Poland, Sweden, Denmark, I beg them to give me their hand and already we greet one another, we embrace one another, we are as brothers. It is the same spirit that enlivens us, the same soul which animates us.

I no longer encounter this fanaticism which took on the language of religion to stir up nation against nation and to drag out disputes and dissent; I no longer hear those war cries which stirred up vengeance and hatred; if we still kill one another, it is at least without animosity.

Our manner of studying is almost uniform. Spanish schools resemble German schools. There we form the same pupils, there we learn, too, how to distinguish between the false and the true, how not to dismiss as mere opinion what is not strictly of faith. Superstition hides herself and Religion shows herself: Her only fear is to be overlooked.

If I examine society, I find it the same for all Europeans, albeit with some nuances. Sweetness makes up the basis, graciousness the polish. We play the same games, we make the same remarks, we have the same ideas, the same feelings. Women are educated in Naples as in Paris, in London as in Madrid, and they are the delight of a society.

The great wit who plays with words is beginning to be heard no longer. There is only the Italian who keeps his *concetti* and who guards them because they concern his language, about which he is justly passionate.

We seek in all parts any work which carries the imprint of delicateness and genius, and we desire universally that it be written in French; it is the only language we love to speak, and would become the only language, if most Europeans were consulted.

There are no longer any fashions but French fashions. English has great trouble indeed in maintaining its own, which are conserved only through vanity.

We dress in Vienna as in Paris, we have our hair styles in Dresden as in Lyons. The majority of Europeans once spent all morning making themselves ridiculous for the rest of the day. It was a mixture of gothic and modern, a hodgepodge of disparate colours which thwarted age and physiognomy. Now it is taste which presides over all *toilettes*, and the taste is that of Paris. [...]

French civility has found no nation reluctant when it is introduced among different peoples. There is no person who does not like lightness and sincerity.

And so Europe is now a painting, all parts of which are admirably linked; the eye perceives in it a unity which is flattering, an order which is satisfying, from which I conclude that we cannot resist the charms of sweetness and suggestion, and that, the further the years progress, the more French graciousness will dominate, this graciousness which brings pleasantness to the most serious things, just as it brings interest to the most insignificant things.

Louis-Antoine Caraccioli,
Paris, the Model of Foreign Nations, or French Europe (1777).

Galerie des Modes, 'Young Lady of Quality in a Formal Dress, Wearing an Elegant Victory Bonnet' (1778), drawn by Claude-Louis Desrais, engraved by Voysant.[i]

Read the free text in the original language (1777 edition):
http://gallica.bnf.fr/ark:/12148/bpt6k1156961

 **Listen to the free audio book in the original language:**
http://gallica.bnf.fr/ark:/12148/bpt6k1156961/f3.vocal

---

i   https://commons.wikimedia.org/wiki/File:1778-jeune-dame-de-qualite-en-grande-robe.jpg

42. Italy and the Origins of European Culture

Corinne is the heroine of the eponymous novel by Germaine de Staël (1766–1817).[i] She personifies female creative genius. The fictional protagonists allow their author to depict European national characters. Here, Prince Castel-Forte's discourse evokes the Italian roots of modern civilisation. Corinne, who is being crowned at the Capitol, is shown as an almost allegorical character, an incarnation of the cradle of European culture.

I cannot flatter myself on having faithfully represented one of whom it is impossible to form an idea till she herself is known; but her presence is left to Rome, as among the chief blessings beneath its brilliant sky. Corinne is the link that binds her friends to each other. She is the motive, the interest of our lives; we rely on her worth, pride in her genius, and say to the sons of other lands, 'Look on the personation of our own fair Italy. She is what we might be, if freed from the ignorance, envy, discord, and sloth, to which fate has reduced us'. We love to contemplate her, as a rare production of our climate, and our fine arts; a relic of the past, a prophetess of the future; and when strangers, pitiless of the faults born of our misfortunes, insult the country whence have arisen the planets that illumed all Europe, still we but say to them, 'Look upon Corinne'.

Germaine de Staël, *Corinne, or Italy*[ii] (1807).

---

i   https://upload.wikimedia.org/wikipedia/commons/3/33/Madame_de_Staël_en_
     Corinne_1807.jpg
ii   https://www.archive.org/stream/corinneoulitalie01stauoft

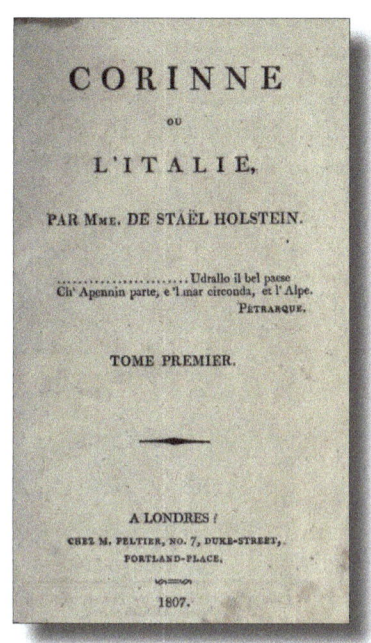

Read the free English text online (1876 edition):
https://books.google.de/books?id=zhbIm7fTqWgC&dq=corin
ne priestess stael&hl=fr&pg=PA28

Read the free text in the original language:
https://www.archive.org/stream/corinneoulitalie01stauoft

43. Europe and French Fashion

Between 1750 and 1758, Anne-Marie Fiquet du Boccage (1710–1802),[i] a writer and translator from Normandy travelled in England, Holland and Italy. She published her letters after her return. This document, a sort of epistolary travel journal, is one of the rare works of this genre to have been written by a woman. Here, she provides a description of fashionable circles in Europe and their social etiquette.

Their morning dresses [the English ladies'] enhance their beauty far more than the French-style outfits that they reserve for evening gatherings, attending court and appearances at the theatre. I do not know why the whole of Europe is so generous as to adopt our fashions, which develop at a speed that makes them impossible to follow, even in our own provinces. Foreigners start wearing them even later, and never in the same way as they have been worn in Paris. Every country has its own language, its morals, its ideas, and should have its own way of dressing, more fitting to its people than any kind of adjusted import. But there are a great number of people here whose splendour, style and substance are borrowed from a multitude of countries.

All things considered, although magnificence is important to the English, they are still a hundred years behind ours, though they try to imitate it and confuse all of Europe.

Anne-Marie du Boccage, *Letters about England, Holland and Italy* (1771).

Read the free text in the original language (1770 edition):
http://gallica.bnf.fr/ark:/12148/bpt6k107281v

🔊 **Listen to the free audio book in the original language:**
http://gallica.bnf.fr/ark:/12148/bpt6k107281v/f2.vocal

---

i   https://commons.wikimedia.org/wiki/File:Anne-Marie_Du_Boccage.jpg

44. Europe Between Decline and Renewal

Friedrich Schlegel (1772–1829),[i] author, translator, literary critic and historian, was a major figure of German Romanticism. His role as an intermediary between cultures comes across in his Journey to France, *published in 1803 in the periodical he edited during his stay in France. He analyses the differences he perceives between Germany and its close neighbour, as well as Europe's situation in the Napoleonic era.*

But is Europe now a continent as thoroughly wretched and as completely disregarded and neglected by nature as, for example, according to the opinion of some philosophical geographers, America supposedly is? No, certainly not; and no historian, no physicist would be willing to agree with such an opinion.

Precisely in the utter disintegration of Europe the beginnings of a higher calling are visible. […]

What in former times was great and beautiful has been so completely destroyed that I do not know how in this sense anyone could maintain that Europe still exists as a whole; rather we only have the surviving remnants, which are the necessary result of that tendency towards division. This latter can be viewed as complete, as it has reached the point of self-destruction. This would therefore seem to have created at least a little room for something new, and precisely because everything has been reduced to ruins, we find we have the materials and means to construct anything, and we ought not to feel daunted about building up and establishing a new world out of this destruction. […]

Let us turn our attention back to the former subject and extend it a little. If those parts of the earth which we very significantly call the Orient and the North represent the visible poles of the principle of good on this earth, whereas everything else appears to be simply empty space, unformed and raw material, distinct weakness and incapacity or even an obstacle which works against this principle, then what really matters

---

i   https://www.flickr.com/photos/ubleipzig/16420319784

here, what everything depends on, is to combine the two. And that may hardly be possible anywhere other than in this continent of ours, which on the face of it has little to recommend it. And in this sense it is probably right to say: the true Europe is yet to emerge.

Friedrich Schlegel, *Journey to France*, 1803.

Allegorical Engraving showing the Treaty of Paris in 1763. Drawing by Monnet, engraved by Jean-Baptiste Tilliard. In the centre: the main countries under the guise of Ancient Goddesses. Title: *Peace Returned to Europe in 1763*. Published in Paris on 21 June of that year.[ii]

Read the free text in the original language (1803 edition):
http://www.ub.uni-bielefeld.de/diglib/aufkl/europa/
europa.htm

---

ii   https://commons.wikimedia.org/wiki/File:Gravure_allégorique_sur_le_traite_de_
      paix_de_1763.jpg

45. The Linguistic Wealth of Europe

In the Project for Perpetual Peace in Europe, *Saint-Pierre evokes the issue of linguistic diversity in Europe and the ensuing problems. He stresses the cultural significance of translation and praises the work of interpreters.*

Two problems have been presented to me. The first is the fact that in Germany, only one language is spoken, while in Europe there are many. To this I respond that if treaties could only be made between sovereigns if they and their subjects share the same language, they could never be negotiated. Yet they are approved every day. How is that possible? It is possible because treaties are negotiated only through deputies, and it is sufficient that deputies representing different nations speak a common language amongst themselves. Moreover, it is common enough to transact with the help of interpreters, without even the deputies comprehending each other's languages.

Charles-Irénée Castel de Saint-Pierre,
Project for Perpetual Peace in Europe (1713).

**Read the free text in the original language
(1713 edition, volume I):**
http://gallica.bnf.fr/ark:/12148/bpt6k86492n?rk=21459;2

**Read the free text in the original language
(1713 edition, volume II):**
http://gallica.bnf.fr/ark:/12148/bpt6k864930?rk=42918;4

46. Spiritual Advent

In 1799, the German romantic writer, Novalis (1772–1801)[i] — or Georg Philipp Friedrich von Hardenberg, to give him his full name — wrote a long fragment, which was only published after his death, and in which he sees the triumph of Christianity as a possible way out of the wars tearing Europe apart.

Now let us turn to the political performance of our own time. The Old World is in conflict with the New and the deficiencies and indigence of present systems of government have been made manifest through terrible phenomena. If only, in politics as in the sciences, closer and more diverse connections and contacts between European States were the first historical purpose of war, if only a new force would come into play to arouse a still-slumbering Europe, if only Europe wished to reawaken. If only a State of States a political theory of knowledge, was imminent. Could hierarchy, this symmetrical basic form of the State, be the principle which unites States as intellectual intuition forms the political self? It is impossible that worldly powers can attain equilibrium, only a third element which is both worldly and transcendental at the same time can fulfil this task. No peace can be concluded between the warring powers; all peace is only an illusion, only a truce. From the standpoint of the politicians and of the general consciousness, a coming-together is inconceivable. Both sides have great and essential claims and must reconcile them, driven by the spirit of the world and of humanity. Both are ineradicable powers of the human heart, here the worship of the Antique, the attachment to a historic system, loving the memorials of our forefathers and the glorious old dynasties of the State, experiencing the joy of obedience; on the other hand, the delightful sensation of Freedom, the boundless expectation of more powerful spheres of activity, the predilection for the new and the young, the

---

i   https://commons.wikimedia.org/wiki/File:Novalis-1.jpg

informal contact with all fellow-citizens, the pride in universal human values, the pleasure of personal rights and of collective ownership and the potent understanding of citizenship. No person would wish to annihilate another, all conquest would be insignificant because the innermost heart of this empire does not lie behind battlements and cannot be stormed.

Who knows if there has been enough of war, but it will never stop if the palm branch is not grasped since only a spiritual power can achieve that end. Blood will stream over Europe until the nations are conscious of the frightful madness into whose spirals they are dragged, until the moment when, hearing and being calmed by holy music, they walk in colourful processions to former altars, take up the works of peace and celebrate peace in a great love-feast, dropping hot tears on the smoking battlefields. Only religion can awaken Europe and secure its people, establishing Christianity, visible on earth in new splendour, in her old office of maintainer of peace.

Novalis, *Christianity or Europe* (1799).

Read the free text in the original language (1799 edition):
http://www.zeno.org/Literatur/M/Novalis/Essay/
Die+Christenheit+oder+Europa

47. The Café: The European Place for Socialising

*For Louis-Antoine Caraccioli (*Paris, the Model of Foreign Nations or French Europe)*, the café seems to have become the quintessential place for socialising in every major European city of the eighteenth century.*

On Cafés

Who would have imagined, two hundred years ago, that a tiny bean from Arabia would lead a multitude of establishments to sprout up across Europe, as practical as they are pleasant, where citizens would gather, foreigners would meet up, and sorrows and woes would be dispelled through innocent pastimes?

Rome, Paris, and London relish the value of such an institution every day. In Venice, even the most distinguished ladies frequent the cafés, proving by their example (which might perhaps be followed on occasion) the extent to which a decent place, open to all respectable people, encompasses pleasures and charms.

We have cafés to thank for an infinite number of connections formed between travellers. In every city, they are a rallying point, and a good many people would find themselves with too much time on their hands if they did not exist.

The Encyclopaedic Dictionary[i] describes them as 'workshops of wit, both good and bad', and one must admit that they often provided a sparring ground for authors. People still remember how full the cafés neighbouring the Comédie Française were, whenever fashionable writers dispensed wisdom on the topics of politics, literature and philosophy there.

Such places still exist, where a foreigner can learn to reel off the latest news, whether true or false, and discern good comedies from bad, provided that the theatrical cabals do not interfere.

---

i   The *Encyclopédie*, compiled by Diderot and D'Alembert, an Enlightenment bestseller, contains a short anonymous article on 'Caffés [sic]' according to which: 'these are places established as the result of the consumption of coffee: all sorts of liquors are imbibed there. They are also workshops of wit, both good and bad'.

Moreover, since cafés are a meeting place for young people who follow the prevailing fashions of the day, one is sure to see the newest crimps, curls and fabrics there.

This is true of cafés across the nations. The travelling Frenchman, keen to see and to be seen, never fails to show himself there, and in the blink of an eye he teaches all who are present how to do up a tie, how to layer their hair, and how to button up a tailcoat.[ii] They stare hungrily at his dashing and elegant figure, while he commands the attention of those who have gathered to listen.

If he does not know the local language, he speaks his own. Those listening whisper in one another's ears that he is truly fascinating, and each one commits to imitating him. That very same day, tailors are summoned, in order to copy the exact style of his outfit.

Fathers, attached to the old way of life, consider these developments to be an attack on their traditions; they grumble and get angry: but their sons are already dressed in the latest fashion—it is a flood that cannot be stopped.

Thus, a thousand times over, in the cafés of Munich and Berlin, of Liège and Rotterdam, after just one glimpse of a Frenchman, his way of dressing, of behaving, and even of existing has been adopted.

Since cafés are the usual haunt of many young people, who have the singular talent of embracing innovation, it is always through them that the elegance of fashions first makes its appearance. It is a delight to see them flying the flag of variety.

At one time, Europeans kept themselves cooped up in their houses; now they show themselves and take joy in conversation. If there are still any proud nations, afraid of compromising themselves by appearing at a café, princes themselves ought to have taught them that one's stature is not harmed at all by doing so. More than once, they have showed up there incognito on their travels, although everyone recognised them. This does not prevent the café from being a pitiable place for those who spend their days languishing there, and unfortunately there are only too many idle folk who subscribe to this way of life. They are there

---

ii   The French term *frac* used here only made its way into the *Dictionary of the Académie Française* in its sixth edition (1832–35): 'An item of clothing for men that only covers the chest at the front, and that ends at the back in two long, more or less narrow tails'.

from ten o'clock in the morning, waiting impatiently for lunchtime, and they return there at three o'clock on the dot, with the prospect of a light supper in view.

Louis-Antoine Caraccioli,
Paris, the Model of Foreign Nations or French Europe (1777).

Read the free text in the original language (1777 edition):
http://gallica.bnf.fr/ark:/12148/bpt6k1156961

 **Listen to the free audio book in the original language:**
http://gallica.bnf.fr/ark:/12148/bpt6k1156961/f3.vocal

48. Happiness in Europe

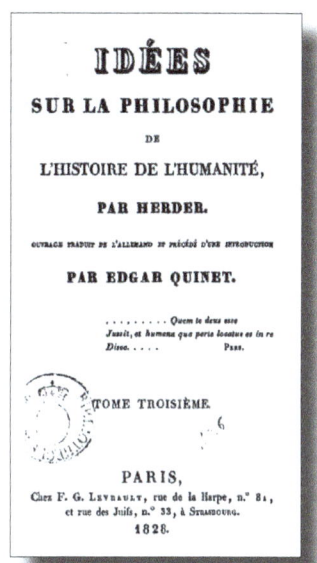

Johann Gottfried Herder ponders the consequences and stakes of eurocentrism.[i] He warns against a form of myopia which could lead one to think of Europe as essentially superior to the rest of the world and estimates that there is not a single way of measuring happiness.

It would be absurdly proud to presume that the inhabitants of all continents would have to be Europeans in order to live happily; for should we have become what we are outside of Europe? [...]

The difference between enlightened and unenlightened, between cultivated and uncultivated peoples, is thus not absolute, but only relative and gradual. Here, the landscape of nations has infinite shading that alters with the variation of location and time; in this case too, as with every landscape, it depends upon the point of view from which you perceive the figures. If we take the concept of European culture as a starting point, it can of course only be found in Europe; if we establish arbitrary distinctions between culture and enlightenment, neither of which, surely, if they are genuine, can exist without the other, then we move even further into cloudcuckooland. But if we keep our feet on this earth and look within its broadest compass at that which Nature, who must know best the purpose and character of its creation, places before our eyes by way of human culture, then this is nothing other than the tradition of raising things to some form of happiness and way of life. This tradition is as universal as the human race. [...]

---

i   http://gallica.bnf.fr/ark:/12148/bpt6k68507x

The glory of many a European people is therefore nothing but vanity, if it seeks to impose itself on all three continents under the banner of so-called Enlightenment, Art and Science.

Johann Gottfried Herder,
Ideas on the Philosophy of the History of Humanity (1784–1791).

Read the free text in the original language (1786 edition):
https://books.google.co.uk/books?id=GegOAAAAQAAJ
&printsec=frontcover

49. The Origins of European Unity

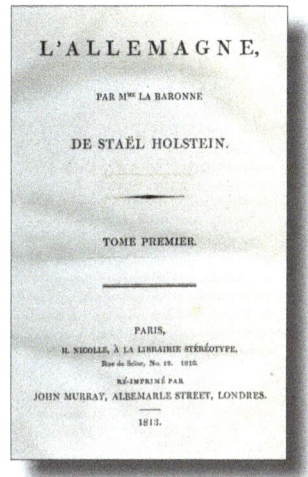

August Wilhelm Schlegel, quoted by his friend Germaine de Staël in her treaty on Germany, De l'Allemagne (1813[i]), evokes the Middle Ages as a period of unity and progress for the whole of Europe.

In those distinguished ages Europe was sole and undivided, and the soil of that universal country was fruitful in those generous thoughts which are calculated to serve as guides through life and in death. Knighthood converted combatants into brethren in arms: they fought in defence of the same faith; the same love inspired all hearts, and the poetry which sung the alliance, expressed the same sentiment in different languages.

Alas ! the noble energy of ancient times is lost: our age is the inventor of a narrow-minded wisdom, and what weak men have no ability to conceive, is in their eyes only a chimera; surely nothing truly great can suceed if undertaken with a grovelling heart. Our times, alas! no longer know either faith or love; how then can hope be expected to remain with them!

Germaine de Staël, *Germany* (1813).

Read the free English text online (1861 edition):
https://books.google.de/books?id=79ETAQAAIAAJ&pg=PA96

Read the free text in the original language (1841 edition):
https://books.google.mu/books?id=pEZbAAAAQAA
J&printsec=frontcover

---

i   https://commons.wikimedia.org/wiki/File:Germaine_de_Staël_-_De_l'Allemagne.jpg

50. European Diversity Through the Foreign Gaze

Following the model of Montesquieu's Persian Letters, *Spaniard José Cadalso (1741–1782)[i] imagines Moroccan visitors in Spain, telling their correspondents about their discoveries as a way of allowing his readers to see their daily life in a new light and teaching them a form of cultural relativity.*

Letter I

Gazel to Ben-Beley

I have managed to stay in Spain following the departure of our Ambassador, as I have wanted to for some time, and as I frequently mentioned in our correspondence during his stay in Madrid. My intention was to travel with purpose, and this is not always possible when travelling in the retinue of great men, particularly Asians or Africans. Let's put it this way: they fail to see beyond the surface of the ground they walk on; their pomp, their lack of history or tradition in studying matters that merit investigation, the number of servants they have, their ignorance of languages, the suspicions they must surely harbour about the countries in which they travel: these and other reasons prevent them from experiencing many things that the less conspicuous, lone traveller can.

I find myself donning the clothes of these Christians, invited into their homes, with a command of their language, and having formed a close friendship with a Christian named Nuño Núñez, a man who has suffered many twists of fate, and practised many professions and lifestyles. He now finds himself isolated from the world, and, as he would say, trapped inside himself. Time flies when I am with him, because he strives to teach me about anything I ask. He does this with such sincerity that sometimes he says to me: 'I do not understand this', and other times he says 'I do not wish to understand this'. Thanks to this

---

i   https://commons.wikimedia.org/wiki/File:Josecadalso.jpg

opportunity I intend to examine not only the court, but all the provinces of the Peninsula. I will observe the customs of these people, noting what they share with other European countries and what is particular to them. I will attempt to rid myself of the many prejudices we Moors hold against Christians, especially against the Spanish. I will take note of everything that surprises me, to be addressed with Nuño, and later relay the good judgement I have formed on the matter to you. [...]

Letter II

From the same to the same

I am still not able to answer your renewed request to pass on the observations which I am making in the capital of this vast monarchy. Do you know how many things are necessary to form a true idea of the country in which one is travelling? It is true that as I have made several trips through Europe, I am better able to so than other Africans or, to put it more correctly, there are fewer obstacles; even so, I have noted such differences between Europeans, that knowing one of the countries in this part of the world is not sufficient to judge the other States. The Europeans do not seem to be neighbours though externally they seem uniform in terms of cuisine, theatres, walks, armies and luxury: their laws, vices, virtues and government are extremely different and so too, as a matter of consequence, are the customs specific to each Nation.

José Cadalso, *Moroccan Letters* (1789).

Read the free text in the original language:
https://es.wikisource.org/wiki/Cartas_marruecas

51. Navigation and Commercial Exchanges

In his History of the Reign of the Emperor Charles V *(1769[i]), which was widely translated and read throughout Europe, William Robertson (1721–1793), a leading figure of the Scottish Enlightenment, presents a wide panorama of the 'progress of society in Europe, from the subversion of the Roman Empire, to the beginning of the sixteenth century'. At several points, he stresses the virtues of commercial and cultural cooperation.*

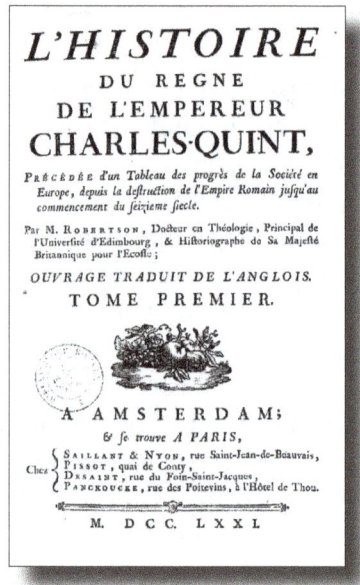

The progress of commerce had considerable influence in polishing the manners of the European nations, and in establishing among them order, equal laws and humanity. The wants of men, in the original and most simple state of society, are so few, and their desires so limited, that they rest contented with the natural productions of their climate and soil, or with what they can add to these by their own rude industry. They have no superfluities to dispose of, and few necessities that demand a supply. Every little community subsisting on its own domestic flock,

---

i   http://gallica.bnf.fr/ark:/12148/bpt6k1161024

and satisfied with it, is either little acquainted with the states around it, or at variance with them. Society and manners must be considerably improved, and many provisions must be made for public order and personal security, before a liberal intercourse can take place between different nations. We find accordingly, that the first effect of the settlement of the barbarians in the Empire, was to divide those nations which the Roman power had united. Europe was broken into many separate communities. The intercourse between these divided States, ceased almost entirely during several centuries. Navigation was dangerous in seas infested by pirates; nor could strangers trust to a friendly reception in the ports of uncivilised nations. Even between distant parts of the same kingdom, the communication was rare and difficult. The lawless rapine of banditti, together with the avowed exactions of the nobles, scarcely less formidable than oppressive, rendered a journey of any length a perilous enterprise. Fixed to the spot in which they resided, the greater part of the inhabitants of Europe lost, in a great measure, the knowledge of remote regions, and were unacquainted with their names, their situations, their climates, and their commodities.

Various causes, however, contributed to revive the spirit of commerce, and to renew, in some degree, the intercourse between different nations. The Italians, by their connection with Constantinople, and other cities of the Greek empire, had preserved in their own country considerable relish for the precious commodities and curious manufactures of the East. They communicated some knowledge of these to the countries contiguous to Italy. But this commerce being extremely limited, the intercourse between different nations was not considerable. The Crusades, by leading multitudes from every corner of Europe into Asia, opened a more extensive communication between the East and West, which subsisted for two centuries; and though the object of these expeditions was conquest and not commerce; though the issue of them proved as unfortunate, as the motives for undertaking them were wild and enthusiastic; their commercial effects, as hath been shown, were both beneficial and permanent. During the continuance of the Crusades, the great cities in Italy, and in other countries of Europe, acquired liberty, and together with it such privileges as rendered them respectable and independent communities. Thus, in every State, there was formed a new order of citizens, to whom commerce presented itself as their proper object, and opened to them a certain path to wealth and consideration. Soon after the close of the Holy War, the mariner's compass was invented, which, by rendering navigation more secure, encouraged it to become more adventurous, facilitated the communication between remote nations, and brought them nearer to each other.

William Robertson,
The History of the Reign of the Emperor Charles V (1769).

Read the free text online (1826 edition):
https://books.google.de/books?id=0594-CKnvO4C
&pg=RA1-PA31

52. Europe and its Long History of Migrations

In his treatise which offers Ideen zur Philosophie der Geschichte der Menschheit *(Ideas on the Philosophy of the History of Humanity, 1784–1791), Johann Gottfried Herder describes the continent's history as a long process largely shaped by the movement of people.*

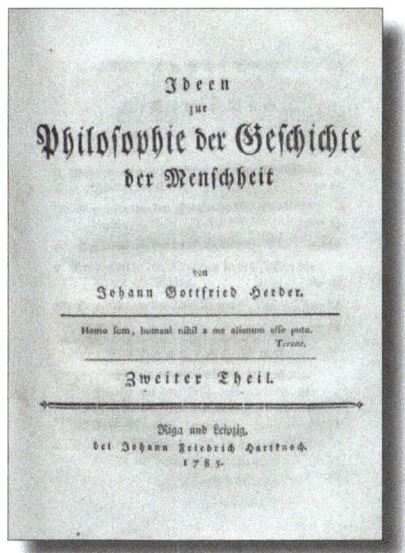

Frontispiece to Johann Gottfried Herder, *Ideen zur Philosophie der Geschichte der Menschheit* (Riga, 1785).[i]

And thus at last, because of the part played by the long migration of peoples over land, in this small continent the beginnings of a great alliance of nations have been established, which the Romans had already unknowingly prepared through their conquests and which could hardly come into being anywhere other than here. In no other part of the world has there been such a mingling of peoples as in Europe; nowhere have they changed their place of habitation, and with it their way of life and customs, so markedly and with such frequency. In many countries it

---

i   http://www.deutschestextarchiv.de/book/show/herder_geschichte02_1785

would now be difficult for the inhabitants, especially some families and individuals, to say from which race or people they come: whether they descend from Goths, Moors, Jews, Carthaginians, Romans, or from Gauls, Celts, Burgundians, Franks, Normans, Saxons, Slavs, Finns, or Illyrians, and how their blood has mixed in the long sequence of their ancestors. Down the centuries the ancient original formation of several European nations has been tempered and altered by a hundred causes, and without this fusion it is unlikely that Europe's universal spirit could ever have been woken.

Johann Gottfried Herder,
Ideas on the Philosophy of the History of Humanity (1784–1791).

Read the free text in the original language (1786 edition):
https://books.google.co.uk/books?id=GegOAAAAQAAJ
&printsec=frontcover

53. Union in Diversity

Dealing with the history of Charles V, Robertson[i] also considers the situation of the main European states at the beginning of the sixteenth century. He starts by inviting us to celebrate our differences whilst recognising what unites us.

As the institutions and events which I have endeavoured to illustrate formed the people of Europe to resemble each other, and conducted them from barbarism to refinement, in the same path, and by nearly equal steps; there were other circumstances which occasioned a difference in their political establishments, and gave rise to those peculiar modes of government, which have produced such variety in the character and genius of nations.

William Robertson,
The History of the Reign of the Emperor Charles V (1769).

Read the free text in the original language (1826 edition):
https://books.google.de/books?id=0594-
CKnvO4C&lpg=RA1-PA31&dq=william robertson pirates
navigation&hl=fr&pg=RA1-PA44

---

i   https://commons.wikimedia.org/wiki/File:William_Robertson_(historian).jpg

54. Europe, a Political Whole

One of the ways of showing Europe's unity, in spite of all that makes it diverse, is to underline the way in which it reacts, as one, to certain events, be they happy or tragic—one example would be the impact of the 1755 Lisbon earthquake on thinkers throughout the continent. Here, in 1746, Diego de Torres Villarroel (1693–1770) imagines an allegorical Europe weeping at the death of King Philip V of Spain.

Sonnet CLXIII

What is this? Clio weeps, her torn hair let down,
Wretched, impatient, inconsolable,
Upon her magnificent, rose-tinged temples
Doleful cypress branches form a crown.
Europe the Superb, the Celebrated,
The Prosperous, the Loving and Joyful,
A second Jerusalem, lies sorrowful,
Alone, deserted and devastated.
What is this? Sad is the air, the sun mournful,
And the Heavens' startlingly bright domain,
In turns appears pale, and then dark as the abyss.
What turmoil is this? What horror? What pain?
What labyrinth makes dark our world? What is this?
What else could it be! Dead is King Philip of Spain!

Diego de Torres Villarroel,
'Sonnet', in *The Muse's Distractions* (1751).

Read the free text in the original language:
http://www.cervantesvirtual.com/obra/sonetos--8/

55. What Are Europeans Like?

In his Amusing and Moral Letters *(1767) Louis-Antoine Caraccioli allows himself to make some observations on the manners of his times in an epistolary form. For him Europe cannot accommodate the high-mindedness of pride. A free life is too much liked there for those who despise the human race to be held in any regard. One of his characters distinguishes the behaviour of Europeans by finding an apposite animal to represent the inhabitants of different nations.*

Midnight is striking, and I am now leaving Lord *** with whom I have had supper. He has just travelled through Europe which he has viewed cooly, in accordance with the character of his nation. He is nonetheless very witty, and could even pass for a Frenchman, if his physiognomy did not herald a foreigner. He claims that, apart from a few nuances, the manners of all Europeans resemble each other.

   He compares the French to squirrels, the Italians to foxes, the Germans to camels, the English to leopards, and to elephants the Spanish.

Louis-Antoine Caraccioli,
Amusing and Moral Letters (1767).

Read the free text in the original language (1767 edition):
https://books.google.co.uk/books?id=rm0PAAAAQAAJ
&printsec=frontcover

56. To Be Cosmopolitan

In 1785 the Journal of a Tour to the Hebrides with Samuel Johnson *was published by his friend, Scotsman James Boswell (1740–1795),[i] on the basis of travel notes taken in the summer and autumn of 1773. The preface contains this declaration by an authentic cosmopolitan who had visited numerous European nations.*

I am, I flatter myself, completely a citizen of the world. In my travels through Holland, Germany, Switzerland, Italy, Corsica, France, I never felt myself from home; and I sincerely love 'every kindred and tongue and people and nation'.

James Boswell,
Journal of a Tour to the Hebrides (1785).

Read the free text in the original language (1876 edition):
https://books.google.co.uk/books?id=po8EAQAAIAAJ
&printsec=frontcover

---

i   https://commons.wikimedia.org/wiki/File:James_Boswell_by_Sir_Joshua_
     Reynolds.jpg

57. French Style in Europe

Louis-Antoine Caraccioli notes that the success of French style in the whole of Europe, be it in the field of fashion, furniture or hairdressing, has consequences in matters of identity and appearance for Europeans from other nations, but also an impact on France's trade balance.

Could one deny that there are truly Parisian German women, and that commerce is an efficient way of making Europeans French?

Louis-Antoine Caraccioli,
Paris, the Model of Foreign Nations, or French Europe (1777).

Read the free text in the original language (1777 edition):
http://gallica.bnf.fr/ark:/12148/bpt6k1156961

Listen to the free audio book in the original language:
http://gallica.bnf.fr/ark:/12148/bpt6k1156961/f3.vocal

58. The Balance of Power and Future Peace

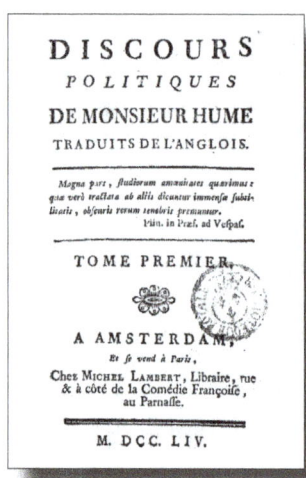

In 1752, in an essay on European equilibrium that was destined to become famous (Of the Balance of Power),[i] *the Scottish philosopher, David Hume, evokes past European wars and his desire for the relationship between different powers to develop in such a way as to guarantee peace, rather than provoke future conflicts.*

In the general wars, maintained against this ambitious power, Great Britain has stood foremost; and she still maintains her station. Beside her advantages of riches and situation, her people are animated with such a national spirit, and are so fully sensible of the blessings of their government, that we may hope their vigour never will languish in so necessary and so just a cause. On the contrary, if we may judge by the past, their passionate ardour seems rather to require some moderation; and they have oftener erred from a laudable excess than from a blameable deficiency.

In the *first* place, we seem to have been more possessed with the ancient Greek spirit of jealous emulation, than actuated by the prudent views of modern politics. Our wars with France have been begun with justice, and even, perhaps, from necessity; but have always been too far pushed from obstinacy and passion. The same peace, which was afterwards made at Ryswick in 1697, was offered so early as the year ninety-two; that concluded at Utrecht in 1712 might have been finished on as good conditions at Gertruydenberg in the year eight; and we might have given at Frankfurt, in 1743, the same terms, which we were glad to accept of at Aix-la-Chapelle in the year forty-eight. Here then we see, that above half of our wars with France and all our public debts, are

---

i   http://gallica.bnf.fr/ark:/12148/bpt6k111321p

owing more to our own imprudent vehemence, than to the ambition of our neighbours.

In the *second* place, we are so declared in our opposition to French power, and so alert in defence of our allies, that they always reckon upon our force as upon their own; and expecting to carry on war at our expense, refuse all reasonable terms of accommodation. *Habent subjectos, tanquam suos, viles ut alienos.*[ii] All the world knows, that the factious vote of the House of Commons, in the beginning of the last parliament, with the professed humour of the nation, made the queen of Hungary inflexible in her terms, and prevented that agreement with Prussia, which would immediately have restored the general tranquillity of Europe.

In the *third* place, we are such true combatants, that, when once engaged, we lose all concern for ourselves and our posterity, and consider only how we may best annoy the enemy. To mortgage our revenues at so deep a rate, in wars, where we were only accessories, was surely the most fatal delusion, that a nation, which had any pretention to politics and prudence, has ever yet been guilty of. That remedy of funding, if it be a remedy, and not rather a poison, ought, in all reason, to be reserved, to the last extremity; and no evil, but the greatest and most urgent, should ever induce us to embrace so dangerous an expedient.

These excesses, to which we have been carried, are prejudicial; and may, perhaps, in time, become still more prejudicial another way, by begetting, as is usual, the opposite extreme, and rendering us totally careless and supine with regard to the fate of Europe. The Athenians, from the most bustling, intriguing, warlike people of Greece, finding their error in thrusting themselves into every quarrel, abandoned all attention to sovereign affairs; and in no contest ever took part on either side, except by their flatteries and complaisance to the victor.

Enormous monarchies are, probably, destructive to human nature; in their progress, in their continuance,[iii] and even in their downfall, which never can be very distant from their establishment. The military genius,

---

ii This is an allusion to Tacitus. Otto, rising up against Emperor Galba, complained he and his partisans were treated like slaves, as though they belonged to their oppressor, but were regarded as worthless as though they belonged to someone else.

iii If the Roman Empire was of advantage, it could only proceed from this, that mankind were generally in a very disorderly, uncivilised condition, before its establishment [author's note].

which aggrandized the monarchy, soon leaves the court, the capital, and the centre of such a government: while the wars are carried on at a great distance, and interest so small a part of the State. The ancient nobility, whose affections attach them to their sovereign, live all at court; and never will accept of military employments, which would carry them to remote and barbarous frontiers, where they are distant both from their pleasures and their fortune. The arms of the State, must, therefore, be entrusted to mercenary strangers, without zeal, without attachment, without honour; ready on every occasion to turn them against the prince, and join each desperate malcontent, who offers pay and plunder. This is the necessary progress of human affairs: Thus ambition blindly labours for the destruction of the conqueror, of his family, and of everything near and dear to him. The Bourbons, trusting to the support of their brave, faithful and affectionate nobility, would push their advantage, without reserve or limitation. These, while fired with glory and emulation, can bear the fatigues and dangers of war; but never would submit to languish in the garrisons of Hungary or Lithuania, forgot at court, and sacrificed to the intrigues of every minion or mistress, who approaches the prince. The troops are filled with Cravates[iv] and Tartars, Hussars and Cossacks; intermingled, perhaps, with a few soldiers of fortune from the better provinces: And the melancholy fate of the Roman emperors, from the same cause, is renewed over and over again, till the final dissolution of the monarchy.

David Hume, 'Essay VII. Of the Balance of Power' (1752).

Read the free text in the original language (1784 edition):
https://books.google.de/books?id=vl3CuC2TUN8C&pg=PA359

---

iv   Croats.

59. A Republic of the Wise

One of the major scientific questions to occupy Enlightenment thinkers was the observation of the transit of Venus. In 1761 and 1769, scientists from different countries studied the phenomenon and communicated their conclusions and interrogations to other members of the academic and intellectual community, as Cadalso (1741–82) recollects here in his posthumous Moroccan Letters.

Did astronomers from every country not come together to observe the transit of Venus across the surface of the sun? Do all of the academies of Europe not share their astronomical observations, their experiments in physics and their advances in all the sciences? Let every nation, then, mark out four or five of their most illustrious, least preoccupied, most active and most hardworking men, and let these men work on the annals of their respective homelands. Afterwards, let the works produced by the efforts of each nation be combined, and from this we shall be able to write a true universal history.

José Cadalso, *Moroccan Letters* (1789).

Read the free text in the original language:
https://es.wikisource.org/wiki/Cartas_marruecas

60. Europe's Future in the Slow Lane?

Jean-Charles-Léonard Simonde de Sismondi (1773–1842)[i] evokes cultural transmissions. He salutes the role of Arab Spain in the propagation of texts and ideas throughout Europe. If Athens has lost its glory, and Rome too, does it not follow that an unknown civilisation could one day shine with a greater light?

Who may say that Europe itself, whither the empire of letters and of science has been transported; which sheds so brilliant a light; which forms so correct a judgment of the past, and which compares so well the successive reigns of the literature and manners of antiquity, shall not, in a few ages, become as wild and deserted as the hills of Mauritania, the sands of Egypt, and the valleys of Anatolia? Who may say, that in some new land, perhaps in those lofty regions, whence the Orinoco and the river of the Amazons have their source, or, perhaps, in the impregnable mountain-fastness of New Holland,[ii] nations with other manners, other languages, other thoughts, and other religions, shall not arise, once more to renew the human race, and to study the past as we have studied it ; nations who, hearing with astonishment of our existence, that our knowledge was as extensive as their own, and that we, like themselves, placed our trust in the stability of fame, shall pity our impotent efforts, and recall the names of Newton, of Racine, and of Tasso, as examples of the vain

---

i   https://commons.wikimedia.org/wiki/File:Jean_Charles_de_Sismondi.jpg
ii   Former name of Australia.

struggles of man to match that immortality of glory, which fate has refused to bestow?

Jean-Charles-Léonard Simonde de Sismondi,
Historical View of the Literature of the South of Europe (1813).

Read the free English text online (1871 edition):
https://books.google.co.uk/books?id=KrJIAQAAMAAJ
&pg=PA62

Read the free text in the original language (1837 edition):
https://books.google.fr/books?id=LLnJzFIoWcoC
&&printsec=frontcover

61. The Union of Philosophers

The ideal of a cross-frontier union, thanks to communications between scientists, but also, more widely, between well disposed individuals, is set out by Germaine de Staël at the end of the third part of her major treatise Germany *(1813).*

After all, there yet remains something truly beautiful and moral, which ignorance and emptiness cannot enjoy: this is the union of all thinking men, from one end of Europe to the other. Often they have no mutual relations; often they are dispersed to a great distance from each other; but when they meet, a word is enough for recognition. It is not this religion, or that opinion, or such a sort of study; it is the veneration of truth that forms their bond of union. Sometimes, like miners, they dig into the foundations of the earth, to penetrate the mysteries of the world of darkness in the bosom of eternal night; sometimes they mount to the summit of Chimborazo, to discover, at the loftiest point of the globe, some hitherto unknown phenomena; sometimes they study the languages of the East, to find in them the primitive history of man; sometimes they journey to Jerusalem, to call forth from the holy ruins a spark, which reanimates religion and poetry; in a word, they truly are the people of God; they who do not yet despair of the human race, and wish to preserve to man the dominion of reflection.

Germaine de Staël, *Germany* (1813).

Read the free English text online (1814 edition):
https://books.google.co.uk/books?id=2fITMg2Nm9IC&dq=stael germany eternal night&pg=RA1-PA284

Read the free text in the original language (1841 edition):
https://books.google.mu/books?id=pEZbAAAAQAAJ &printsec=frontcover

62. A New Idea in Europe

On 3 March 1794 — or 13 Ventôse ('the windy month') of year II according to the revolutionary calendar — just a few months before dying on the scaffold, the radical deputy Louis-Antoine-Léon de Saint-Just (1767–1794),[i] who was 26 years old, suggested the French example could lead the way in bringing happiness to the people beyond its borders. Here he is addressing the French parliament, or 'Convention', as it was known at that time.

The peoples of Europe are being wilfully misled about what is going on here in France. Your debates are being misrepresented. But powerful laws cannot be misrepresented. They strike at the heart of foreign countries like unstoppable bolts of lightning. Let Europe learn that you will no longer countenance people being miserable and poor, that you will no longer countenance any oppressor! May this example bear fruit across the land; may the love of virtue and happiness spread throughout the world! Happiness is a new concept in Europe.

Louis-Antoine-Léon de Saint-Just,
Speech, 3 March 1794.

Read the free text in the original language (1834 edition):
https://books.google.co.uk/books?id=ETsuAAAAMAAJ
&printsec=frontcover

---

i   https://commons.wikimedia.org/wiki/File:Saint_Just.jpg

63. A Humanitarian Vision

According to Condorcet (1743–1794), the true philosopher has one essential aim: to improve the fate of all mankind, without distinction of nationality, religion or race. Anti-slavery movements are an example of what one should promote.

The philosophers of different nations embracing, in their meditations, the entire interests of man, without distinction of country, of colour, or of sect, formed, notwithstanding the difference of their speculative opinion, a firm and united phalanx against every description of error, every species of tyranny. Animated by the sentiment of universal philanthropy, they declaimed equally against injustice, whether existing in a foreign country, or exercised by their own country against a foreign nation. They impeached in Europe the avidity which stained the shores of America, Africa, and Asia with cruelty and crimes. The philosophers of France and England gloried in assuming the appellation, and fulfilling the duties, of *friends* to those very Negroes whom their ignorant oppressors disdained to rank in the class of men. The French writers bestowed the tribute of their praise on the toleration granted in Russia and Sweden, while Beccaria refuted in Italy the barbarous maxims of Gallic jurisprudence.

Marie-Jean-Antoine-Nicolas de Caritat, Marquis de Condorcet,
Outlines of an Historical View of the Progress of the Human Mind (1794).

Read the free English text online (1795 edition):
https://books.google.co.uk/books?id=SLs8AAAAYAAJ
&dq=condorcet america africa asia&pg=PA256

Read the free text in the original language (1822 edition):
https://books.google.de/books?id=hRIPAAAAQAAJ
&printsec=frontcover

64. Towards the Balance of Powers

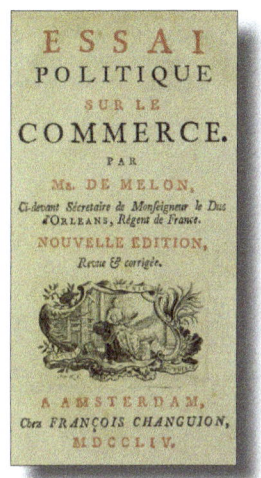

In 1734, Jean-François Melon (1675–1738),[i] who was born in Tulle, published his Essai Politique sur le Commerce *(Political Essay on Commerce) defending mercantilism and sketching out ideas the physiocrats later developed. He points out the true economic value of a balance of powers in Europe.*

The spirit of Peace has finally shone on our Europe. For as long as it reigns, a fair balance will ever stop a Power from rising sufficiently through its conquests to be feared; and should any momentary interests trouble this happy harmony, the Victor will no longer be able to hope to extend his borders: all must unite to stop his dangerous progress and a Nation will no longer be able to grow except through the wisdom of its internal government.

Jean-François Melon, *A Political Essay on Commerce* (1734).

Read the free text in the original language (1735 edition):
https://books.google.co.uk/books?id=7phaAAAAcAAJ
&printsec=frontcover

---

i   https://commons.wikimedia.org/wiki/File:Melon_-_Essai_politique_sur_le_
commerce,_1754_-_5717500.tif

65. Towards Cultural Uniformity?

In his 1771 Considerations on the Government of Poland[i], *Rousseau talks about the similarities he sees between people of different countries.*

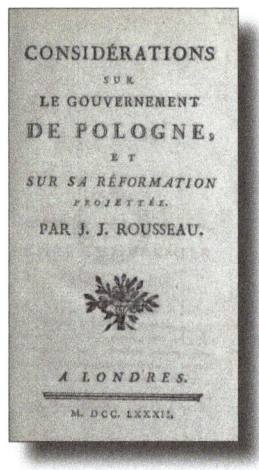

These days, whatever else one may say, there are no longer any Frenchmen, Englishmen, Germans or Spaniards, there are only Europeans. Everyone has the same tastes, the same passions, the same customs, for none of them has been moulded by national institutions.

Jean-Jacques Rousseau,
Considerations on the Government of Poland (1771).

Read the free text in the original language (1782 edition):
http://gallica.bnf.fr/ark:/12148/bpt6k9626109r

 **Listen to the free audio book in the original language:**
http://gallica.bnf.fr/ark:/12148/bpt6k9626109r/f7.vocal

---

i   http://gallica.bnf.fr/ark:/12148/bpt6k9626109r/f7.highres

66. Europe and Africa

The fictitious correspondent imagined by Cadalso makes comments likely to provoke incomprehension in a number of his compatriots at the time his book was published. Yet he sets out truths: in some societies, like the Moroccan one, an important place is granted, in pedagogy, to essential aspects which the educators of members of the European aristocracy had a tendency to neglect.

Famous anti-slavery medallion drawn by Josiah Wedgwood, *c*.1787.[i]

Letter XLII

Nuño to Ben-Beley

According to the account that Gazel has given me of you, I know that you are an upstanding gentleman who lives in Africa, and you will have equally discerned from the account of me that he will have personally given you, that I too am an upstanding gentleman living in Europe. I believe that nothing more is necessary for us to form a good opinion of one another. We respect each other though we are yet to have the occasion to meet; as long as we address each other as such, we will be friends.

---

i   https://commons.wikimedia.org/wiki/File:Wedgwood_-_Anti-Slavery_Medallion_-_Walters_482597.jpg

This young man's demeanour and the knowledge that he was raised at your hand compel me to leave Europe and voyage to Africa, where you reside. I wish to spend time around an African scholar, as I swear that I am weary of European scholars, save a few who live in Europe as if they were in Africa. I would be grateful if you could tell me what methods you used and what you hoped to achieve through Gazel's education. In truth, I find him uncultured in his understanding, but he is inclined to do good; and as I hold all the world's learning on matters of virtue in very low regard, I long for a dozen or so tutors such as yourself to come and take charge of the education of our young people, instead of leaving it in the hands of their European counterparts. They let their students' hearts wander astray, only to fill their heads with prattle of glory, French courtesies, Spanish vanity, Italian arias and other similarly 'perfect' and 'important' things; things that are no doubt very valuable, given the amount of money spent on teaching them, but which nevertheless seem so very inferior to the maxims that I have seen Gazel himself put into practice.

José Cadalso, *Moroccan Letters* (1789).

Read the free text in the original language:
https://es.wikisource.org/wiki/Cartas_marruecas

67. Fulfilling Nature's Aims

In his Idea for a Universal History from a Cosmopolitan Point of View
*(1784), Immanuel Kant formulates a series of propositions he sees as having
the potential to help man to understand both his individual destiny and world
evolution. He ponders the notion of progress and sets out the idea of Nature's
'hidden plan' which should be taken into account in order to arrive at a society
of nations guided by moral rules.*

It is possible to consider the history of the human species in general
as the execution of a hidden plan of Nature, intended to bring about a
constitution which is perfect both internally and, for this very purpose,
also externally, as the only condition in which nature can fully develop
all its tendencies as they are present in mankind. […]

The States are now already in such a delicately poised relationship
with one another that not one of them can yield in inner cultivation
without losing in power and influence with regard to other States; for
this reason the preservation of this purpose of Nature, if not actually
its progress, is more or less secured by the very ambitions of the States'
intentions. Furthermore: civic freedom can now not very well be
encroached upon, without the disadvantages of this making itself felt
in all industries – above all, trade – but also in a decrease in the powers
of the State in its exterior relations. This freedom is in fact gradually
growing. If one prevents the citizen from pursuing prosperity in any
way he sees fit provided it can co-exist with the freedom of others, one
inhibits the liveliness of general business and in turn, at the same time,
the powers of the whole. Hence, the personal restrictions on doing
as one pleases are increasingly being lifted, and universal religious
freedom is given way to. Thus arises gradually, as delusion and
wilfulness recede, *Enlightenment*, as a great good which the human race,
if it only understands what is to its own advantage, must extract even
from its rulers' selfish aims of expansion. This Enlightenment, however,
and with it a certain amount of sympathy which the enlightened human
being cannot avoid investing in the good that he fully understands,
will gradually make its way up to the thrones, and exert influence

upon the very principles of government. Although, for example, our world leaders for the moment have no money to spare for State-funded education and for anything at all which pertains to that which is best in the world, because all funds have already been allocated to the coming war, they will still find that it is to their own advantage at least not to hamper the independent efforts of their people in this undertaking, feeble and slow as they are. Eventually war itself will gradually become not only such a contrived undertaking, its outcome so uncertain on both sides, but also such a hazardous one given the long-term consequences which the State suffers in the form of a constantly growing burden of debt (a new invention), which it seems will never be written off; and at the same time the influence which every shock to the State in our part of the world, which is so interconnected by its trade, has on other States will become so noticeable, that, driven by their own insecurity, though without legal standing, they will offer themselves as adjudicators, and thus from afar set everything on the path to becoming a large political body in the future, of which the world so far has no example to put forward. Although this political body is, for now, only present in rough outline, a feeling has nevertheless begun to stir in all its limbs, each of which is concerned with the preservation of the whole. This gives hope that, after several revolutions of reorganisation, that which is Nature's highest purpose – a universal, cosmopolitan condition as the womb in which all the original tendencies of the human species may be developed – will one day come into being.

Immanuel Kant,
Idea for a Universal History from a Cosmopolitan Point of View (1784).

Read the free text in the original language (1784 edition):
http://gutenberg.spiegel.de/buch/-3506/1

68. Governing Europe?

On Saint-Helena, the Comte de Las Cases retranscribed the deposed Emperor Napoleon's thoughts and remarks. His notes for 24 August 1816 show the importance of certain structures to bring about the unity Napoleon would have liked to achieve.

He then went over what he would have proposed for posterity, the interests, enjoyment and wellbeing of the European association. He would have wanted the same principles and system throughout; a European code, a European high court to redress all errors as ours does those of our own tribunals. The same currency franked in different places; the same weights, the same measures, the same laws, etc. etc. Europe, he said, would thus shortly have become a single nation, and everyone wherever they travelled, would always have found themselves in their common homeland.

Emmanuel-Auguste-Dieudonné-Marius de Las Cases,
Memorial of Saint-Helena, 24 August 1816 (1822–23).

Read the free text in the original language (1823 edition):
https://babel.hathitrust.org/cgi/pt?id=nyp.33433069328346

69. Know the World and Make it a Better Place

According to Condorcet, the discovery of America had a huge impact on the whole of humanity and on the freedom of people in Europe and elsewhere. As he writes, he hopes for a pacific republican future.

It is in this epoch only of the progress of the human mind, that man has arrived at the knowledge of the globe which he inhabits; that he has been able to study, in all its countries, the species to which he belongs, modified by the continued influence of natural causes, or of social institutions; that he has had an opportunity of observing the productions of the earth, or of the sea, in all temperatures and climates. And accordingly, among the happy consequences of the discoveries in question, may be included the resources of every kind which those productions afford to mankind, and which, so far from being exhausted, men have yet no idea of their extent; the truths which the knowledge of those objects may have added to the sciences, or the long received errors that may thereby have been destroyed; the commercial activity that has given new life to industry and navigation, and, by a necessary chain of connection, to all the arts and all the sciences: and lastly, the force that free nations have acquired from this activity by which to resist tyrants, and subjected nations to break their chains, and free themselves at least from feudal despotism. But these advantages will never expiate what the discoveries have cost to suffering humanity, till the moment when Europe, abjuring the sordid and oppressive system of commercial monopoly, shall acknowledge that men of other climates, equals and brothers by the will of nature, have never been formed to nourish the pride and avarice of a few privileged nations; till, better informed respecting its true interests, it shall invite all the people of the earth to participate in its independence, its liberty, and its illumination. Unfortunately, we have yet to learn whether this revolution will be the honourable fruit of the advancement of philosophy, or only, as we have hitherto seen, the shameful consequence of national jealousy, and the enormous excesses of tyranny.

Marie-Jean-Antoine-Nicolas de Caritat, Marquis de Condorcet, *Outlines of an Historical View of the Progress of the Human Mind* (1794).

Read the free English text online (1795 edition):
https://books.google.co.uk/books?id=SLs8AAAAYAAJ&dq=con
dorcet america africa asia&pg=PA188

Read the free text in the original language (1822 edition):
https://books.google.de/books?id=hRIPAAAAQAAJ
&printsec=frontcover

70. An End to Wars in Europe?

Benjamin Constant (1767–1830),[i] in On the Spirit of Conquest and Usurpation in Respect of European Civilisation *(1814), includes a chapter entitled 'On the Spirit of Conquest in the Present State of Europe'. He returns to an idea that is dear to him: that the age of war is (or ought to be) definitively over.*

Nowadays, a government which wanted to push a European people to war and conquests would thereby be committing a gross and deadly anachronism. It would be working to give its nation an impulse against nature. As none of the motives which moved the men of earlier ages to face so many dangers, to bear so many wearying things still exists for the men of our own times, other motives would need to be found, drawn from the present state of our civilisation; they would need to be roused to combats by that same love of pleasures which, left to its own devices, would dispose them only to peace. Our age, which measures everything in terms of utility, and which, when one seeks to move it on from this sphere, sets irony against real or specious enthusiasm, would not readily sate itself on sterile glory which it is no longer our custom to prefer above all others. Pleasure should replace this glory and pillage replace triumph. One shudders to think what the military spirit would become, were it founded solely on these motives.

Benjamin Constant,
On the Spirit of Conquest and Usurpation in Respect of European Civilisation[ii] (1814).

---

i   https://www.flickr.com/photos/fdctsevilla/4189272153
ii   http://gallica.bnf.fr/ark:/12148/bpt6k1157300

DE L'ESPRIT

DE CONQUÊTE

ET

DE L'USURPATION,

DANS LEURS RAPPORTS

AVEC LA CIVILISATION EUROPÉENNE.

Par BENJAMIN DE CONSTANT-REBECQUE,
MEMBRE DU TRIBUNAT, ÉLIMINÉ EN 1802, CORRESPONDANT DE LA
SOCIÉTÉ ROYALE DES SCIENCES DE GOTTINGUE.

TROISIÈME ÉDITION,

REVUE ET AUGMENTÉE.

PARIS,

Chez { LE NORMANT, Libraire, rue de Seine, n° 8;
H. NICOLLE, Libraire, même rue, n° 12.

M. DCCC. XIV.

Read the free text in the original language (1814 edition):
http://gallica.bnf.fr/ark:/12148/bpt6k1157300

 **Listen to the free audio book in the original language:**
http://gallica.bnf.fr/ark:/12148/bpt6k1157300/f4.vocal

71. Visions of the Future

According to those who knew him, Napoleon Bonaparte (1769–1821),[i] imprisoned on Saint-Helena, was conscious of having failed in his aim to conquer, but continued to affirm that the future of Europe demanded greater unity.

The impulse has been given, and I do not believe that after my fall and the disappearance of my system there will be any major equilibrium possible in Europe other than by the agglomeration and confederation of the great peoples.

> Napoleon Bonaparte, quoted by Las Cases,
> *Memorial of Saint-Helena* (1822–23).

Read the free text in the original language:
https://babel.hathitrust.org/cgi/pt?id=nyp.33433069328346

---

i   https://commons.wikimedia.org/wiki/File:Napoleon_crop.jpg

72. A Critique of Eurocentrism

A reader of Voltaire's Micromégas, *Cadalso is writing here to his friend, the poet Iriarte. In his mocking observation he illustrates the circulation of images, texts and ideas throughout Europe, and the awareness Spanish intellectuals had of the advances necessary for Spain to keep up with the rest of Europe where Enlightenment ideals were more prevalent.*

In the most frequented coffeehouse in one of the main cities of the Planet we call Saturn, one often sees the most authentic gazettes being read. The following piece of news appeared in the final paragraph of one of them a short while ago, and it has become the topic of all conversations across the political, military, scholastic, and legal domains in those lands. It has fallen into my hands through the magic of a witch who lives a door down from me, and it reads as follows:

> In a tiny globe made of solids and liquids that circles around the great and only luminary, there is a small area called Europe, inhabited by some minute and exceedingly despicable insects called men. One almost uncultured and unpopulated section of said Europe is known as Spain.

Letter from José Cadalso to Tomás de Iriarte (*c*.1774).

Read the free text in the original language:
http://www.cervantesvirtual.com/obra-visor/cartas-de-cadalso-a-toms-de-iriarte-0/html/01de8e8a-82b2-11df-acc7-002185ce6064_2.html

73. Political Hegemony and European Union

On Saint-Helena, Napoleon evokes the pan-European dimension of his political project in front of Las Cases and shows that, for him, the project of a great empire presented numerous challenges and had considerable potential, but also that it was an unprecedented historical occasion.

Napoleon Bonaparte dictating his memoirs to generals Montholon and Gourgaud in the presence of Grand-Marshal Bertrand and Count de Las Cases.[i]

One of my great plans was the rejoining, the concentration of those same geographical nations which have been disunited and parcelled out by revolution and policy. There are dispersed in Europe, upwards of 30,000,000 of French, 15,000,000 of Spaniards, 15,000,000 of Italians, and 30,000,000 of Germans; and it was my intention to incorporate these people each into one nation. It would have been a noble thing to have advanced into posterity with such a train, and attended by the blessings of the future ages. I felt myself worthy of this glory!

After this summary simplification, it would have been possible to indulge the chimera of the *beau idéal* of civilisation. In this state of things, there would have been some chance of establishing, in every country, a unity of codes, principles, opinions, sentiments, views and interests. Then, perhaps, by the help of the universal diffusion of knowledge, one might have thought of attempting, in the great European family, the

---

i   https://commons.wikimedia.org/wiki/File:Napoléon_Ier_dictant_ses_mémoires.jpg

application of the American Congress, or the Amphictyons of Greece.[ii] What a perspective of power, grandeur, happiness, and prosperity, would thus have appeared!...

Napoleon Bonaparte on 11 November 1816, quoted by Las Cases in *Mémorial de Sainte-Hélène. Journal of the Private Life and Conversations of the Emperor Napoleon at Saint Helena* (1822–23).

Read the free English text online (1823 edition):
https://books.google.co.uk/
books?id=mLFCAAAAYAAJ&pg=PA67

Read the free text in the original language (1823 edition):
https://babel.hathitrust.org/cgi/pt?id=nyp.33433069328346

---

ii   In Ancient Greece, the Council of the Amphictyons, at Delphi, decided on public affairs; it was also supposedly proposed as a model by the French King Henry IV, who brought peace to a France riven by religious war, but who would be assassinated in 1610.

74. Europe without Frontiers

If numerous authors show the exchanges which peace makes possible, the Marquis de Pezay manages here to find an epigrammatic expression of the happy consequences of such relations: 'A nation rarely goes to war against a nation with which it often trades'.

Beyond the advantage the traveller gains from the perfection of the roads traced almost throughout Europe, this multiplicity of paths gives rise to an idea yet more satisfying than the very ease procured.

The traveller's ease is nothing: it is almost the disadvantageous side, compared with the other seriously useful aims which improvement in major routes affects. It would indeed not be particularly serious if rocks were still to rise up before cossetting chariots, if fewer rich men allowed themselves to be cossetted in such carriages, and a greater number of them were, on horseback, to exercise their slumbering limbs and also their minds. But there is a true good, a good from which a thousand others derive, that is the universal appeal addressed to all the tradesmen in the universe by the simplicity of travelling along these routes and, by way of consequence, exchanging goods; it is the chain of society strengthened and extended by the power of mutual needs, satisfied by the ease of this exchange; it is the multiplicity of the ties to which it gives birth between people; it is the weeding out or at very least the weakening of national prejudice through commerce between Nations; it is courtesy in behaviour, perfection in the arts and in peace. A people rarely fights another people with which it has regular commercial exchanges.

Alexandre-Frédéric-Jacques de Masson de Pezay,
Helvetic, Alsatian and Franc-Comtois Vigils (1771).

75. Multiple Influences

A true European, with ties to Switzerland, the United Kingdom and Italy, a close friend of Germaine de Staël and other members of the Groupe de Coppet, Jean-Charles-Léonard Simonde de Sismondi, when he undertakes to present the literature of southern Europe, recognises the importance of several traditions he regrets not to be able to master completely. His book gives a considerable place to Arab philosophy, poetry and science as motors of cultural development.

I am ignorant of the Oriental languages, and yet it was the Arabian which, in the middle ages, gave a new impulse to the literature of Europe, and changed the course of the human mind. I am ignorant, likewise, of the Slavonic tongues, and yet the Russian and the Polish boast of literary treasures, a brief account of which I could present to my readers only on the authority of others. Amongst the Teutonic languages I am acquainted with the English and the German alone; and the literature of Holland, Denmark and Sweden, is only accessible to me in an imperfect manner, through the medium of German translations. Still, the languages of which I shall give a summary account, are those in which there exist the greatest number of masterpieces, and which at the same time possess the most original and novel spirit; and, indeed, even with these restrictions, the ground which I intend to traverse is still sufficiently extensive.

Jean-Charles-Léonard Simonde de Sismondi,
Historical View of the Literature of the South of Europe (1813).

Read the free English text online (1871 edition):
https://books.google.co.uk/books?id=KrJIAQAAMAAJ&dq=si
smondi europe racine&hl=fr&pg=PA26

Read the free text in the original language (1837 edition):
https://books.google.fr/books?id=LLnJzFIoWcoC
&&printsec=frontcover

76. What Future for Europe?

Swiss intellectual Johannes von Müller (1752–1809)[i] was an active correspondent. In a 1778 letter he speaks of the importance of history to attempt to understand what the future has in store. He is conscious that the balance of power in Europe and beyond is about to shift.

It is unbelievable how beautiful history is, but the historian who must write about all aspects of Administration, requires all the knowledge that a king should have. Burgoyne's misfortune should serve as a lesson to historians as times are coming when Europe may no longer be at the centre of the world. Thus, small, local events which are only important to local princes, will be banished from history, while Ancient and Modern history will both be regarded in the same way. As far as imminent new revolutions which will occur in the future, they will be a resource for political maxims, which sooner or later, will find an application. Europe is perhaps playing her last act, and we shall be more able in the future

---

i   https://commons.wikimedia.org/wiki/File:JvMueller.jpg

than we are at present, to appreciate each incident of the great drama which is unfolding and to assign to it its rightful place in our annals.

Johannes von Müller,
Letter 80, January 1778 in *Collected Works*, 1812.

Read the free text in the original language :
http://gallica.bnf.fr/ark:/12148/bpt6k9633042c

Listen to the free audio book in the original language:
http://gallica.bnf.fr/ark:/12148/bpt6k9633042c/f9.vocal

77. The Character of Modern Exchanges

Benjamin Constant, in The Liberty of the Ancients Compared with that of the Moderns *(1819), a speech delivered at the Royal Athenaeum in Paris, reflects on commercial trade as an expression of European relations which, in his opinion, has supplanted war.*

Thanks to advancements in our enlightenment, the very division of Europe into multiple States is more perceived than real. Whereas in the past each nation formed an isolated family, the natural born enemy of other families, a body of men now exists under different names, and with different means of social organisation, yet homogenous in nature. This body is strong enough that it has nothing to fear from barbarian hordes. It is enlightened enough that it sees war as a burden. It heads invariably towards peace.

This difference brings yet another with it. War existed before trade, for war and trade are merely two different ways of reaching the same goal: possessing what we desire. Trade is merely a tribute paid to the power of the possessor by he who aspires to possess. It is an attempt to obtain by mutual consent that which we can no longer hope to win through violence. The idea of trade would never have occurred to any man who was always the strongest. It is experience which, by proving to him that war—namely, the use of his own strength against another's— exposes him to resistance and failure in a variety of forms, leads him to resort to trade, which is a gentler and surer method of engaging another to agree to what serves his own interests. War is a matter of impulse, trade of calculation. But it follows that there must come a time when trade will replace war. That time has come.

I do not mean to suggest that merchant peoples did not exist among the ancients. But these peoples were, in a sense, exceptions to the general rule. [...] Where once trade was a happy accident, today it is the norm, the sole aim, the universal tendency, the very lifeblood of nations. They want peace, and with this peace prosperity, a prosperity with industry as its source. With each passing day war becomes a less effective way of fulfilling their desires. The fortunes it offers to individuals and nations can no longer equal the results achieved by peaceful work and regular exchange. In the time of the ancients, a successful war contributed to public and private wealth through slaves, tributes, and the sharing out of territory. In modern times, a successful war will invariably cost more than it is worth.

In conclusion, thanks to trade, religion, and the moral and intellectual progress of mankind, there are no longer slaves in European nations. Free men must apply themselves to all types of profession to provide for all of society's needs.

Benjamin Constant,
The Liberty of the Ancients Compared with that of the Moderns (1819).

Read the free text in the original language (1819 edition):
http://etienne.chouard.free.fr/Europe/Docs/Constant_
Benjamin_Liberte_anciens_modernes_1819.pdf

78. Unity through Measures

According to Laplace, a mathematician and senator who defended the propagation of a single system of weights and measures in Napoleon's realm, the same standards should provide the basis for a common culture promoted by the Emperor's actions.

Thanks to his Genius, the whole of Europe will soon form a single immense family, united by the same religion, the same legal code and the same weights and measures.

Pierre-Simon Laplace,
An Exposition of the System of the World, 4th ed. (1813).

Read the free text in the original language (1813 edition):
https://archive.org/details/expositiondusys01laplgoog

79. The Franco-German Couple as the Pillars of Peace in Europe

Victor Hugo (1802–1885),[i] French Romantic poet, novelist, dramatist and politician, published his narration of travels through Germany undertaken in 1842. He was to give a second longer version in 1845 with the title of The Rhine, Letters to a Friend. *In it, he reflects on the specificities of the Franco-German relationship and its importance for peace in Europe.*

So what is left of all this old world? What is still standing in Europe? Only two nations: France and Germany. Well that could be enough. France and Germany are essentially Europe. Germany is the heart; France is the head. Germany and France are essentially civilisation. Germany feels; France thinks. Feeling and thought make up civilised man. Between the two peoples, there is an intimate connection, an undeniable consanguinity. They were born from the same sources; together they fought against the Romans; they are brothers in the past, brothers in the present, brothers in the future. They were shaped the same way. They are not insular, they are not conquerors; they are the true sons of the European soil. [...]

For the universe to be balanced, there need to be in Europe, like the double keystone of the continent, two great Rhine States, both fertilised and closely bound by this regenerating river; one northern and eastern, Germany, buttressed by the Baltic, the Adriatic and the Black sea, with Sweden, Denmark, Greece and the Danube principalities as its girders; the other, southern and western, buttressed by the Mediterranean and the Ocean, with Italy and Spain as its stanchions. [...]

Europe needs to defend itself. The old Europe, which was a complicated assembly, has been demolished; Europe now is of a much

---

i   https://commons.wikimedia.org/wiki/File:Victor_Hugo_001.jpg

simpler shape. It is essentially made up of France and Germany, a double centre from which the group of nations must take strength to the North as to the South. The alliance of France and Germany is Europe's constitution. Germany backed by France holds Russia in check; France with friendly support from Germany stops England. The disunion of France and Germany is Europe's dislocation. Germany, turned to France in hostility, opens the door to Russia; France, turned to Germany in hostility, allows England in. [...]

Fortunately, neither France nor Germany is selfish. They are two sincere, selfless and noble peoples, formerly nations of knights, and now nations of thinkers; formerly great by the sword, now great by the mind. Their present will not belie their past; the mind is no less generous than the sword. Here is the solution: abolish any motive for hatred between the two peoples; close the wound made in 1815; remove the traces of a violent reaction; return to France what God gave her, the Rhine's left bank. [...]

Within a given time, France will have its share of the Rhine and of its natural frontiers.

This solution will constitute Europe, will save human sociability and found definitive peace. All peoples will profit from this. Spain, for instance, which has remained illustrious, could be powerful once more. England would like Spain to be the market for her products, the fulcrum for her navy; France would like Spain to be the sister of her influence, her politics and her civilisation. It will be up to Spain to choose: to continue going downwards or to start rising once more; to be an annex of Gibraltar, or to be the buttress of France. Spain will choose grandeur. That is, we believe, the inevitable future for the continent, already visible and distinct in the sunset of things to come. Once the motive for hatred has disappeared, Europe needs fear no people. Germany will only need a shake of its mane and a roar to the East; France will just have to open its wings and shake its lightning bolt to the West. The formidable accord between lion and eagle will make the world obey.

Make no mistake regarding what we believe: at all times, Europe must watch out for revolutions and be strengthened against wars, but we also think that if no incident outside natural previsions were to trouble the nineteenth century's majestic march, civilisation, already saved from so many storms and reefs, will distance itself every day more from the Charybdis of war and the Scylla of revolution.

This may be utopian, but do not forget that utopias, when they have the same aim as humanity—that which is good, just and true—are the facts of the next century. Some men say: *This will be*; and other men say: *This is how*. The first seek; the others find. Perpetual peace was a dream until the day the dream became a railway and covered the earth in a solid, tenacious and living network. Watt complements the Abbé de Saint-Pierre. [...]

For perpetual peace to be possible and to pass from theory to reality, two things were necessary: a vehicle for the rapid service of interest, and a vehicle for the rapid exchange of ideas; in other terms, uniform, unitary and sovereign transport, and a common language. The universe now possesses these two means which tend to delete the borders of empires and intelligences. The first is the railway; the second is the French language.

Such, in the nineteenth century, for all peoples on the road to progress, are the two means of communication, that is to say of civilisation, that is to say of peace. You ride in a railway carriage and you speak French. [...]

Let us resume. We believe, if the future brings what we await, that the chances of war and revolution will diminish day by day. We do not think they will ever disappear completely. Universal peace is a hyperbola; the human race follows its asymptote. The law of humanity is to follow this radiant asymptote. During the nineteenth century, all nations are marching that way or soon will, even Russia, even England.

Victor Hugo, *The Rhine* (1842–1845).

Read the free text in the original language (1884 edition):
http://gallica.bnf.fr/ark:/12148/bpt6k37469b

Listen to the free audio book in the original language:
http://gallica.bnf.fr/ark:/12148/bpt6k37469b/f3.vocal

Bibliography

Boccage, Marie-Anne du, *Œuvres, Lettres sur l'Angleterre, la Hollande et l'Italie*, Lyon, Frères Périsse, 1770, vol. III, p. 13, p. 37.
http://gallica.bnf.fr/ark:/12148/bpt6k107281v (French edition)
http://gallica.bnf.fr/ark:/12148/bpt6k107281v/f2.vocal (French audio book)

Boswell, James, Boswell's *Life of Johnson: Including their Tour to the Hebrides*, ed. John Wilson Croker, London, John Murray, 1876, pp. 269–270.
https://books.google.co.uk/books?id=po8EAQAAIAAJ&printsec=frontcover

Cadalso, José, *Cartas marruecas*, Biblioteca virtual Miguel de Cervantes.
https://es.wikisource.org/wiki/Cartas_marruecas (Spanish edition)

Cadalso, José, *Letter from José Cadalso to Tomás de Iriarte*, c.1774, Biblioteca Nacional de Madrid, Ms. K, 356.
http://www.cervantesvirtual.com/obra-visor/cartas-de-cadalso-a-toms-de-iriarte-0/html/01de8e8a-82b2-11df-acc7-002185ce6064_2.html (Spanish transcription)

Caraccioli, Louis-Antoine, *Paris, le modèle des nations étrangères ou l'Europe française*, Paris, Duchesne, 1777, pp. 1–3, pp. 52–58, pp. 84–98, pp. 169–78, pp. 246–52, pp. 350–58.
http://gallica.bnf.fr/ark:/12148/bpt6k1156961 (French edition)
http://gallica.bnf.fr/ark:/12148/bpt6k1156961/f3.vocal (French audio book)

Caraccioli, Louis-Antoine, *Lettres récréatives et morales sur les mœurs du temps*, Paris, Nyon, 1767, vol. II, p. 289, pp. 297–98.
https://books.google.co.uk/books?id=rm0PAAAAQAAJ&printsec=frontcover (French edition)

Condorcet, Marie-Jean-Antoine-Nicolas de Caritat, Marquis de, *Outlines of an Historical View of the Progress of the Human Mind*, London, J. Johnson, 1795, pp. 188–190 and pp. 256–257.
https://books.google.co.uk/books?id=SLs8AAAAYAAJ&dq=condorcet america africa asia&pg=PA256
https://books.google.de/books?id=hRIPAAAAQAAJ&printsec=frontcover (1822 French edition)

Constant, Benjamin, *De l'esprit de conquête et de l'usurpation dans leurs rapports avec la civilisation européenne*, Paris, Le Normant, 1814, pp. 17–18.
http://gallica.bnf.fr/ark:/12148/bpt6k1157300 (French edition)
http://gallica.bnf.fr/ark:/12148/bpt6k1157300/f4.vocal (French audio book)

Constant, Benjamin, *De la liberté des anciens comparée à celle des modernes, Collection complète des ouvrages, publiés sur le gouvernement représentatif et la constitution actuelle, ou Cours de politique constitutionnelle*, vol. IV, Paris, Béchet et Rouen, Béchet fils, 1820, pp. 245–48.
http://etienne.chouard.free.fr/Europe/Docs/Constant_Benjamin_Liberte_anciens_modernes_1819.pdf (French edition)

Coyer, Gabriel, *Voyage d'Italie et de Hollande*, Paris, Veuve Duchesne, 1775, 2 vol. in 1 vol., vol. II, p. 53.
http://gallica.bnf.fr/ark:/12148/bpt6k103467z (French edition)

François-Ignace d'Espiard de La Borde, *The Spirit of Nations*, London, Lockyer Davis, 1753, pp. 4–6 and 366–369.
https://books.google.co.uk/books?id=7YjTkxx12qAC&lpg=PA4&dq=espiard de la borde earth three equator&hl=fr&pg=PA4
https://books.google.co.uk/books?id=o2Q9AQAAMAAJ&printsec=frontcover (French edition)

Gibbon, Edward, *The History of the Decline and Fall of the Roman Empire*, Project Gutenberg, 1997.
https://www.gutenberg.org/files/25717/25717-h/25717-h.htm

Graffigny, Françoise de, *Letters of a Peruvian Princess*, translated by Francis Ashmore, London, Harrison and Co., 1787, pp. 29–30.
https://books.google.co.uk/books?id=Gd1IAQAAMAAJ&dq=aza capa inca men peru&hl=fr&pg=PA29
http://gallica.bnf.fr/ark:/12148/bpt6k62721455 (1777 French edition)
http://gallica.bnf.fr/ark:/12148/bpt6k62721455/f4.vocal (French audio book)

Herder, Johann Gottfried, *Ideen zur Philosophie der Geschichte der Menschheit*, Riga and Leipzig, Johann Friedrich Hartenoch, 1786.
https://books.google.co.uk/books?id=GegOAAAAQAAJ&printsec=frontcover (German edition)

Hugo, Victor, 'Le Rhin' (1842–1845), in *Œuvres complètes, Le Rhin II*, Paris, Hetzel/Quentin, 1884, pp. 370–71, pp. 372–73, pp. 318–19, p. 420, pp. 421–22, p. 423, p. 424, pp. 425–26.
http://gallica.bnf.fr/ark:/12148/bpt6k37469b (French edition)
http://gallica.bnf.fr/ark:/12148/bpt6k37469b/f3.vocal (French audio book)

Hume, David, *Political Discourses*, Edinburgh, R. Fleming, 1752, 2nd ed., pp. 27–28, p. 29.
https://books.google.co.uk/books?id=fR9YAAAAcAAJ&pg=PA27

Hume, David, 'Essay VII. Of the Balance of Power', in *Essays and Treatises on Several Subjects*, 2 vols., London, T. Cadell, 1784, vol. I, pp. 359–52.
https://books.google.de/books?id=vl3CuC2TUN8C&pg=PA359

Iriarte, Tomás de, 'Fábula XLI: El té y la salvia', *Fábulas Literarias*, Madrid, Imprenta Real, 1782, p. 80.
http://albalearning.com/audiolibros/iriarte/41te.html (Spanish edition)
http://albalearning.com/SONIDO/iriarte/albalearning-41te_iriarte.mp3 (Spanish audio book)

Jaucourt, Louis de, 'Europe', in *Encyclopédie ou Dictionnaire raisonné des sciences, des arts et des métiers*, 17 vols., Paris, 1751–1765, vol. VI, pp. 211–212.
https://fr.wikisource.org/wiki/L'Encyclopédie/1re_édition/Volume_6 (French edition)

Kant, Immanuel, *Zum ewigen Frieden. Ein philosophischer Entwurf*, Project Gutenberg, 2014.
http://www.gutenberg.org/files/46873/46873-h/46873-h.htm (German edition)

Kant, Immanuel, *Idee zu einer universellen Geschichte in weltbürgerlicher Absicht, Gesammelte Schriften*, herausgegeben von der königlich preußischen Akademie der Wissenschaften und Nachfolgern, Berlin 1900, vol. VIII, pp. 17–31.
http://gutenberg.spiegel.de/buch/-3506/1 (German edition)

Laplace, Pierre-Simon, *Exposition du système du monde*, 4th ed., Paris, Veuve Courcier, 1813, vol. I, p. 142.
https://archive.org/details/expositiondusys01laplgoog (French edition)

Las Cases, Emmanuel-Auguste-Dieudonné-Marius de: *Journal of the Private Life and Conversations of the Emperor Napoleon at Saint Helena*, Boston, Wells and Lilly, 1823, vol. IV, pp. 66–67.
https://books.google.co.uk/books?id=mLFCAAAAYAAJ&pg=PA67
https://babel.hathitrust.org/cgi/pt?id=nyp.33433069328346 (French edition)

Leprince de Beaumont, Marie, *Magasin des adolescentes ou Dialogues entre une sage gouvernante, et plusieurs de ses élèves de la première distinction*, Londres, 1760, vol. II, pp. 117–18.
http://gallica.bnf.fr/ark:/12148/bpt6k5773041g (French edition)
http://gallica.bnf.fr/ark:/12148/bpt6k5773041g/f2.vocal (French audio book)

Leszczynski, Stanislas, *Entretien d'un Européen avec un insulaire du Royaume de Dumocala*, Nancy, 1752, pp. 60–64.
http://gallica.bnf.fr/ark:/12148/bpt6k84469n (French edition)

Masson de Pezay, Alexandre-Frédéric-Jacques de, *Les soirées Helvétiennes, Alsaciennes et Franc-Comtoises*, Amsterdam 1771, pp. 310–11.
https://books.google.co.uk/books?id=G5sOAAAAQAAJ&printsec=frontcover

Melon, Jean-François, *Essai Politique sur le Commerce*, Amsterdam, François Changuion, 1735, p. 102.
https://books.google.co.uk/books?id=7phaAAAAcAAJ&printsec=frontcover (French edition)

Montesquieu (Charles-Louis de Secondat, Baron of La Brède et of Montesquieu), *The Spirit of Laws*, 2 vols., Glasgow, J. Duncan & Son, 1793, vol. II, pp. 54–56.
https://books.google.co.uk/books?id=uxBVAAAAYAAJ&pg=PA54
http://classiques.uqac.ca/classiques/montesquieu/de_esprit_des_lois/partie_4/esprit_des_lois_Livre_4.pdf (1748 French edition)

Montesquieu, *Persian Letters*, 3rd ed., 2 vols., translated by John Ozell, London, J. Tonson, 1736, vol. II, pp. 182–187.
https://books.google.co.uk/books?id=rAE6AAAAcAAJ&printsec=frontcover
https://fr.wikisource.org/wiki/Lettres_persanes (1873 French edition)

Muratori, Louis-Antoine, *Della pubblica felicità, oggetto de' buoni principi*, Lucca, 1749.
https://archive.org/details/bub_gb_3SRnd5k3HHsC (Italian edition)

Müller, Jean de [Johannes von Müller], *Letter 80* in *Sämmtliche Werke*, Tübingen, Cotta, 1812, vol. XIII, p. 264.
http://gallica.bnf.fr/ark:/12148/bpt6k9633042c (German edition)
http://gallica.bnf.fr/ark:/12148/bpt6k9633042c/f9.vocal (German audio book)

Nivernais, Louis-Jules Barbon Mancini-Mazarini, Duke of, *Fables de Mancini-Nivernois* publiées par l'auteur, Paris, Didot, 1796, vol. II, p. 142.
https://archive.org/details/fablesdemancinin02nive (French edition)

Novalis, *Die Christenheit oder Europa* (1799).
http://www.zeno.org/Literatur/M/Novalis/Essay/Die+Christenheit+oder+Europa (German edition)

Robertson, William, *The History of the Reign of the Emperor Charles V. With a View of the Progress of Society in Europe, from the Subversion of the Roman Empire, to the Beginning of the Sixteenth Century*, London, Jones & Company, 1826, p. 31, pp. 44–45.
https://books.google.de/books?id=0594-CKnvO4C&pg=RA1-PA31

Rousseau, Jean-Jacques, *Considérations sur le gouvernement de Pologne*, Londres, [s.n.], 1782.
http://gallica.bnf.fr/ark:/12148/bpt6k9626109r (French edition)
http://gallica.bnf.fr/ark:/12148/bpt6k9626109r/f7.vocal (French audio book)

Rousseau, Jean-Jacques, *Œuvres*, Paris, Defer de Maisonneuve, 1793, p. 413.

Rousseau, Jean-Jacques, *A Lasting Peace Through the Federation of Europe*, translated by C. E. Vaughan, London, Constable and Company Ltd., 1917, pp. 40–50.
http://lf-oll.s3.amazonaws.com/titles/1010/0147_Bk.pdf
http://gallica.bnf.fr/ark:/12148/bpt6k2051816 (French edition)

Rousseau, Jean-Jacques, *Jugement sur la paix perpétuelle,* in J.-J. Rousseau, *Œuvres complètes*, Paris, Dalibon, 1826, vol. VI, pp. 440–47.
http://gallica.bnf.fr/ark:/12148/bpt6k2051816 (French edition)

Saint-Just, Louis-Antoine-Léon de, *Œuvres*, Paris, Prévot, 1834, p. 218.
https://books.google.co.uk/books?id=ETsuAAAAMAAJ&printsec=frontcover (French edition)

Saint-Pierre, Charles-Irénée Castel de, *Projet pour rendre la paix perpétuelle en Europe*, Utrecht, Antoine Schouten, 1713, vol. I, preface, pp. 112–13, pp. 268–69, p. 283 ; vol. II, pp. 127–30, pp. 308–09, pp. 335–36.
http://gallica.bnf.fr/ark:/12148/bpt6k86492n?rk=21459;2 (French edition, vol. I)
http://gallica.bnf.fr/ark:/12148/bpt6k864930?rk=42918;4 (French edition, vol. II)

Simonde de Sismondi, Jean-Charles-Léonard, *Historical View of the Literature of the South of Europe*, 2 vols., New York, Harper and Brothers, 1871, vol. I, p. 62–63.
https://books.google.co.uk/books?id=KrJIAQAAMAAJ&dq=sismondi europe racine&hl=fr&pg=PA62
https://books.google.fr/books?id=LLnJzFIoWcoC&&printsec=frontcover (1837 French edition)

Schiller, Friedrich, 'Ode an die Freude', in *Schillers Werke, Nationalausgabe*, ed. Julius Petersen, *Gedichte*, Weimar, Böhlau, 1943, vol. I, pp. 169–72.
https://de.wikisource.org/wiki/Ode_an_die_Freude (German edition)

Schlegel, Friedrich, 'Reise nach Frankreich', in *Europa. Eine Zeitschrift*, ed. F. Schlegel, Ersten Bandes erstes Stück, Frankfurt/M., Friedrich Wilmans, 1803, pp. 31–34.
http://www.ub.uni-bielefeld.de/diglib/aufkl/europa/europa.htm (German edition)

Schlegel, August Wilhelm, 'Abriss von den europäischen Verhältnissen der deutschen Literatur', in A.W. Schlegel, *Kritische Schriften*, Berlin, Georg Reimer, 1828, pp. 1–14.

Staël, Germaine de, *De la littérature considérée dans ses rapports avec les institutions sociales*, Paris, Crapelet, 1800, vol. I, pp. 296–312.
http://gallica.bnf.fr/ark:/12148/bpt6k61078256/f2.image (French edition)
http://gallica.bnf.fr/ark:/12148/bpt6k61078256/f2.vocal (French audio book)

Staël, Germaine de, *Corinne, or Italy*, translated by Isabel Hill with metrical versions of the odes by L.E. Landon, New York, Albert Mason, 1876, p. 28.
https://books.google.de/books?id=zhbIm7fTqWgC&dq=corinne priestess stael&hl=fr&pg=PA28
https://www.archive.org/stream/corinneoulitalie01stauoft (1807 French edition)

Staël, Germaine de, *Germany*, 2 vols., Murray translation, Boston, Houghton, Mifflin and Company, 1814, vol. I, pp. 284–285.
https://books.google.co.uk/books?id=2fITMg2Nm9IC&dq=stael germany eternal night&pg=RA1-PA284
https://books.google.mu/books?id=pEZbAAAAQAAJ&printsec=frontcover (1841 French edition)

Supplément à l'Encyclopédie, Amsterdam, Rey, 1776, vol. I, p. 93.
http://gallica.bnf.fr/ark:/12148/bpt6k50550x/f1.image (French edition)

Sully, Maximilien de Béthune, Duke of, *Memoirs*, 5th ed., 6 vols., Dublin, R. Marchbank, 1781, vol. VI, pp. 66, 72–5 and 81, pp. 89–90.
https://books.google.co.uk/books?id=9OI9AQAAMAAJ&lpg=PA313&dq=sully vervins memoirs&hl=fr&pg=PA66
https://books.google.de/books?id=t-iAVIeyd8UC&printsec=frontcover (1778 French edition)

Torres Villarroel, Diego de, *Viaje fantástico del Gran Piscátor de Salamanca*, Biblioteca Virtual Universal, [n.d.].
http://biblioteca.org.ar/libros/132245.pdf (Spanish edition)

Torres Villarroel, Diego de, 'Sonetos', in *Entretenimientos del Numen. Varias poesías*, Salamanca, Impr. Antonio Joseph Villagordo y Alcaraz, 1751, vol. VII, [n.p.].
http://www.cervantesvirtual.com/obra/sonetos--8/ (Spanish edition)

Villers, Charles de, *Constitutions des trois villes libres-anséatiques, Lubeck, Brêmen et Hambourg, avec un Mémoire sur le rang que doivent occuper ces villes dans l'organisation commerciale de l'Europe*, Leipzig, Brockhaus, 1814, pp. 98–143.
https://books.google.co.uk/books?id=deBYAAAAcAAJ&printsec=frontcover (French edition)

Voltaire, *Essai sur les mœurs et l'esprit des nations*, 1756, in *Œuvres de Voltaire*, ed. M. Beuchot, Paris, Lefèvre, 1829–1834, vol. XVIII, pp. 488–90.
http://gallica.bnf.fr/ark:/12148/bpt6k375239 (French edition)

Voltaire, *Le siècle de Louis XIV*, 1751, in *Œuvres complètes de Voltaire*, Paris, Garnier, 1878, vol. XIV, p. 159–75.
https://fr.wikisource.org/wiki/Le_Siècle_de_Louis_XIV (French edition)

You may also be interested in:

Tolerance
The Beacon of the Enlightenment
Translated by Caroline Warman, et al.

http://dx.doi.org/10.11647/OBP.0088
https://www.openbookpublishers.com/product/418

Denis Diderot
'Rameau's Nephew' — 'Le Neveu de Rameau'
A Multi-Media Bilingual Edition
Edited by M. Hobson. Translated by K.E. Tunstall and
C. Warman. With music specially performed by the Conservatoire
national supérieur de musique et de danse de Paris

http://dx.doi.org/10.11647/OBP.0098
https://www.openbookpublishers.com/product/498

L'idée de l'Europe au Siècle des Lumières
Textes réunis par Rotraud von Kulessa et Catriona Seth

http://dx.doi.org/10.11647/OBP.0116
https://www.openbookpublishers.com/product/610

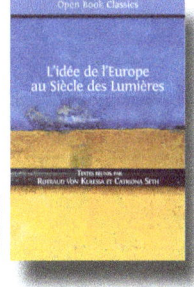

www.ingramcontent.com/pod-product-compliance
Lightning Source LLC
Chambersburg PA
CBHW072356030726
47505CB00014B/1856